TEDDY ROOSEVELT
AMERICAN ROUGH RIDER

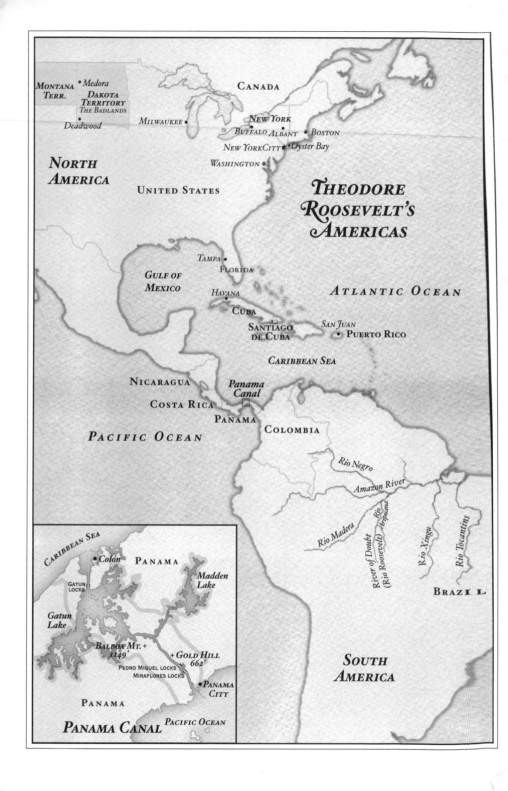

MONTANA TERR.
DAKOTA TERRITORY
*Medora
THE BADLANDS
*Deadwood

CANADA

MILWAUKEE *

NEW YORK
BUFFALO ALBANY * BOSTON
NEW YORK CITY* *Oyster Bay
WASHINGTON ⊛

NORTH AMERICA

UNITED STATES

THEODORE ROOSEVELT'S AMERICAS

TAMPA *
FLORIDA
GULF OF MEXICO
HAVANA *

ATLANTIC OCEAN

CUBA
SANTIAGO DE CUBA
SAN JUAN
* PUERTO RICO

CARIBBEAN SEA

NICARAGUA
Panama Canal
COSTA RICA
PANAMA

COLOMBIA

PACIFIC OCEAN

Rio Negro

Amazon River

Rio Madera

Rio Madeira

River of Doubt
(Rio Roosevelt)

Rio Arípuanã

Rio Xingu

Rio Tocantins

BRAZIL

SOUTH AMERICA

CARIBBEAN SEA
*Colón
PANAMA
GATUN LOCKS
Madden Lake
Gatun Lake
BALBOA MT. +
1149'
PEDRO MIGUEL LOCKS
MIRAFLORES LOCKS
+ GOLD HILL
662'
*PANAMA CITY
PANAMA

PANAMA CANAL
PACIFIC OCEAN

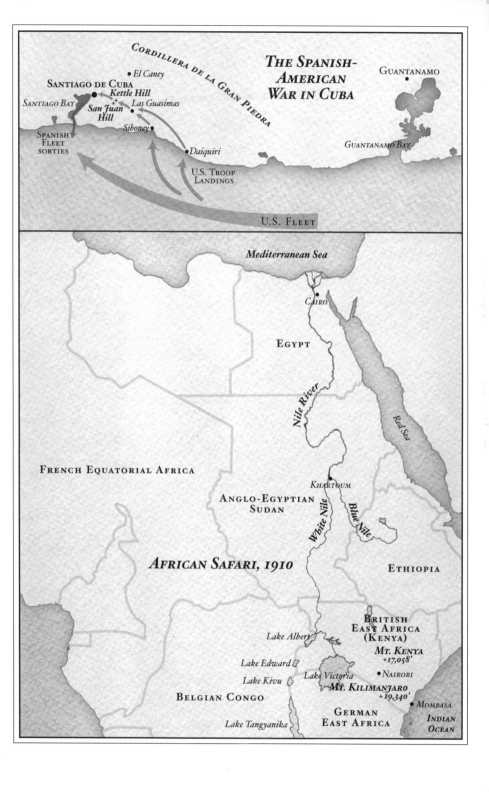

THE SPANISH-
AMERICAN
WAR IN CUBA

CORDILLERA DE LA GRAN PIEDRA

• El Caney

SANTIAGO DE CUBA
Kettle Hill
SANTIAGO BAY
San Juan
Hill
Las Guasimas
SPANISH
FLEET
SORTIES
Siboney•
• Daiquiri

GUANTANAMO
•

GUANTANAMO BAY

U.S. TROOP
LANDINGS

U.S. FLEET

Mediterranean Sea

CAIRO•

EGYPT

Nile River

Red Sea

FRENCH EQUATORIAL AFRICA

KHARTOUM•

ANGLO-EGYPTIAN
SUDAN

White Nile

Blue Nile

AFRICAN SAFARI, 1910

ETHIOPIA

Lake Albert

BRITISH
EAST AFRICA
(KENYA)

MT. KENYA
+17,058'

Lake Edward

Lake Kivu
Lake Victoria

• NAIROBI

MT. KILIMANJARO
+19,340'

BELGIAN CONGO

• MOMBASA

GERMAN
EAST AFRICA

INDIAN
OCEAN

Lake Tangyanika

Theodore Roosevelt

CONTENTS

TEDDY ROOSEVELT
AMERICAN ROUGH RIDER

DETERMINED TO SUCCEED

FEW AMERICANS HAVE POSSESSED THE DETER-
mination, toughness, and courage of Theodore Roosevelt
or have enjoyed life so fully in so many different ways. He
wrote scholarly books but also hunted lions in Africa.
He hobnobbed with kings and sparred with the heavy-
weight boxing champion of the world. In a relatively
short life he was a police chief, a soldier, a first-rate natural scientist, a state legislator and a governor, a rancher
who captured a gang of horse thieves at gunpoint—and
the twenty-sixth President of the United States.

Yet he did not come by these qualities without effort
or accomplish so much merely by being talented. He

attained courage by overcoming fear, strength by conquering weakness. He could scarcely see without thick glasses, but he became a crack shot and a famous big-game hunter. This was typical. His life is a monument to the ability of the human spirit to rise above obstacles, to the power of mind over matter.

Theodore Roosevelt was born on October 27, 1858, in New York City. His father, Theodore Roosevelt Sr., was a successful merchant who specialized in the importation of glass products. The family was of Dutch ancestry, tracing its roots back to the 1640's, when Klaes Martensen van Roosevelt had settled on Manhattan Island, then the Dutch colony of New Amsterdam. The elder Roosevelt was socially prominent, comfortably wealthy, and also public spirited. He helped found a hospital, the New York Children's Aid Society, and other charitable organizations. A big, handsome, energetic man with a full beard, he was both physically vigorous and intensely idealistic. Young Theodore (the family called him "Teedie") worshiped him, writing in his *Autobiography*: "My father . . .

was the best man I ever knew. He combined strength and courage with gentleness, tenderness, and great unselfishness. He would not tolerate in us children selfishness or cruelty, idleness, cowardice, or untruthfulness." Roosevelt's summary of his father's personality can also serve to sum up his own: "I never knew any one who got greater joy out of living, or any one who more whole-heartedly performed every duty."

The child Teedie, living in the shadow of this powerful but loving figure, absorbed his influence and adopted his values. But nature had played a dreadful trick upon the boy. Besides being born with extremely bad eyesight, he was thin and sickly, afflicted with a long series of childhood diseases. The most serious of these was asthma, which periodically constricted his throat and left him gasping for breath. Asthmatic attacks struck him time after time during his childhood and youth. No treatment helped much, although fresh country air and plenty of rest at least lessened the force of the attacks.

Theodore's physical weakness, however, stimulated

and strengthened other parts of his nature: his love both of the outdoors, which provided the best hope of relief for his asthma, and of books, which he read greedily when illness confined him at home.

In the long run, his puny body provided the inspiration for its own strengthening and development. The elder Theodore worried constantly about his son's health and lavished the most tender care on him during the cruel asthmatic attacks. Yet he feared that the boy might retreat into invalidism or allow himself to find in books a substitute, rather than a supplement, for a life of action and accomplishment. Teedie had been too sickly to attend a regular school; he was educated chiefly by tutors in his own home. There he was surrounded by a loving family. Besides his father and his mother, the former Martha Bulloch, who came from Georgia, he had an older sister, Anna, a younger brother, Elliott, and a younger sister, Corinne. But Theodore had little experience with the rough-and-tumble, the games, the fights, and the friendships of ordinary youngsters.

One day when Teedie was twelve, his father took him aside and said, "You have the mind but not the body, and without the help of the body the mind cannot go as far as it should. You must *make* your body . . . I know you will do it." He bought his son a punching bag, a set of dumbbells, and other gymnastic equipment, and the boy set to work to build up his muscles. He made some progress, but he remained timid. In his few contacts with other boys his own age he often relied on his younger brother to protect him when squabbles arose.

Then, when he was thirteen, an unpleasant incident helped to change his life. Theodore was traveling without his family to a summer resort. Two boys his own age were also on the stagecoach, and they quickly discovered in young Roosevelt an object for easy bullying. When he grew angry and tried to fight back, he found that either of the boys could "not only handle me with easy contempt, but handle me so as not to hurt me much and yet prevent my doing any damage whatever in return."

This humiliating experience convinced Theodore that

5

he must learn to defend himself. He took boxing lessons and eventually won a lightweight contest in "championship" matches sponsored by his instructor. The cheap pewter mug he received as a prize he treasured for years. He also continued with his body-building exercises, and by the time he went to college he was in excellent shape.

To triumph over his feeble body had become so important to him, however, that it made him extremely aggressive. He tended to overstress the importance of strength and courage. In competitive situations he was actually belligerent. It seemed necessary to prove constantly that he was strong and brave, that he could defeat any opponent, accomplish any objective. For example, although he genuinely loved all kinds of wild animals, he took an almost abnormal relish in hunting and killing.

The year he turned fourteen, the Roosevelt family took a trip to Egypt. Traveling up the Nile River, Theodore frequently went off with his shotgun to hunt birds. His diary is full of his exploits. February 4: "Killed a ringed plover." February 5: "Shot a sand chat and an

Egyptian plover and got a bat." February 7: "Killed 17 pigeons."

Along with his athletic endeavors, young Roosevelt remained interested in reading and study. At eighteen he entered Harvard College, where he proved to be an excellent student, curious and hardworking. He was elected to the college honor society, Phi Beta Kappa, and even began, while a senior, the research that resulted in his first book, the scholarly *The Naval War of 1812*. He also participated fully in sports and other activities, working, for example, on the *Crimson*, the college newspaper.

Roosevelt's aggressiveness showed itself even in the classroom. He loved to argue, to challenge the opinions of his professors. "The courses . . . were very cold and uninteresting before Roosevelt came," a fellow student reported. "With his appearance and questionings, things livened up." One day an exasperated professor finally said, "Now look here, Roosevelt, let me talk. I'm running this course."

While at Harvard, Roosevelt met Alice Lee, a blond,

gray-eyed Boston beauty of seventeen. He fell in love at first sight and began to overwhelm the girl with his attentions, even asking her to watch while he fought (unsuccessfully) for the lightweight championship of Harvard. "See that girl?" he said to a friend at a college party. "I am going to marry her. She won't have me, but I am going to have her!" After a year of almost constant persuasion, Alice finally accepted him.

Once they were engaged, he grew absurdly over-protective and jealous. When another young man even talked with her at a dance, he became greatly alarmed. Once he sent off to France for a set of dueling pistols simply because he imagined that another man was trying to steal Alice from him.

They were married in 1880, shortly after his graduation from Harvard. The young couple settled in New York, where Roosevelt enrolled at the Columbia University Law School. But the study of law did not interest him, and he soon dropped out of the school. Politics, on the other hand, fascinated him, and he enthusiastically adopted his father's belief that men of wealth and intelligence should devote themselves to public service.

In the late nineteenth century, New York City politics was dominated by corrupt party bosses who arranged the election of their candidates through political machines. "When I began to make inquiries as to the whereabouts of the local Republican association," Roosevelt later recalled, "the men I knew best . . . laughed at me, and told me that politics was 'low'; that the organizations were not controlled by 'gentlemen'. . . . They assured me that the men I met would be rough and brutal and unpleasant to deal with. I answered that if this were so it merely meant that the people I knew did not belong to the governing class. . . ."

The idealistic Roosevelt promptly joined the local Republican club, attending meetings regularly. The bosses saw the advantage of running a bright, socially prominent young man like Roosevelt for office. Despite the fact that he resolutely refused, if elected, to support the machine, the bosses nominated Roosevelt for state assemblyman. On election day, November 8, 1881, he defeated his Democratic rival by a large majority.

When he reached Albany, the state capital, in January, 1882, the twenty-three-year-old legislator very quickly aroused the ire of the professional politicians. First of all, his appearance and manner irritated them. His cultivated Harvard way of speaking and his fashionable clothes (he would sometimes attend party planning sessions in the evenings in a full-dress suit) led them to write him off as a rich dude, a mere amateur politician. His fondness for talking and arguing also impressed them as unfitting in a young and totally inexperienced lawmaker.

More important, he angered the politicians by trying to remove from office a prominent judge on grounds of corruption and by attacking a bill reducing the taxes paid by a New York elevated-railways company. Yet the professionals soon came to respect, almost to fear, this brash young man. He would not give up, even against heavy odds, and he was already demonstrating an instinct for attracting the attention and support of the public. By the end of his first term he was known all over the state as a leader of the reform element. As a result he was twice re-elected to the assembly, in 1882 and in 1883.

Actually, Roosevelt was no radical. He tended to look down on ordinary workingmen and to oppose bills limiting the rights of businessmen, as long as they conducted their affairs honestly. He voted against a bill reducing the working hours of streetcar conductors, calling it "socialistic." He was also sharply prejudiced against Democrats. He classified "over half" the Democrats in the legislature as "vicious, stupid-looking scoundrels," surely an exaggeration even in a time of "dirty" politics. Revealing his remarkable gift for expressing his thoughts in colorful language, he said that one of his Democratic colleagues had "the same idea of public life . . . that a vulture has of a dead sheep." Too often he saw things as either black or white. Men were either good or bad, honest or crooked. And of course what he believed was

100 percent right; those who opposed him had to be entirely wrong.

Nevertheless, Roosevelt did much good work at Albany. His most notable achievement while a state legislator was a fight against the dreadful conditions in the slums of New York City. There whole families lived in single rooms, barely surviving on the money made in long hours of cigar making. A bill had been introduced outlawing the manufacture of cigars in tenement houses. Originally Roosevelt opposed it as a violation of men's freedom to conduct their businesses however they pleased. But the labor leader Samuel Gompers persuaded him to visit some of these gloomy, unhealthy sweatshops. "The tobacco was stowed about everywhere," Roosevelt discovered, "alongside the foul bedding, and in a corner there were scraps of food. The men, women, and children in this room worked by day and far on into the evening, and they slept and ate there." The aristocratic young lawmaker was converted on the spot. He championed the bill in speeches, helped force it through a reluctant legislature, and then persuaded the hesitant Democratic governor of the state, Grover Cleveland, to sign it into law. It marked Roosevelt's first advance from the position of a gentleman reformer interested only in honest government to that of a real reformer concerned with social justice and human welfare.

CHAPTER 2

THE DAKOTA COWBOY

ON FEBRUARY 13, 1884, ROOSEVELT, THEN AT
the beginning of his third term in the legislature, stood at
a pinnacle of happiness and success. He was winning
increasing respect as a legislator, and he had just received
a telegram announcing the birth of his first child, Alice
Lee. Then fate suddenly struck him a devastating blow. A
second telegram arrived at Albany: both his mother and
his wife were desperately ill. He rushed back to New
York, arriving shortly before midnight, to find them on
the verge of death, his wife from complications resulting
from the baby's birth, his mother from typhoid fever.
Within a matter of hours, both were dead. "For joy or for

sorrow," the stricken man wrote in his diary, "my life has now been lived out."

Of course this was not true; the young man's sense of duty and his driving energy soon reasserted themselves. He returned to his desk at the state capitol. "It was a grim and evil fate," he wrote, "but I have never believed it did any good to flinch or yield for any blow, nor does it lighten the blow to cease from working."

Then in June, Roosevelt was struck another blow, this one political. A presidential election was approaching. Roosevelt was supporting Senator George F. Edmunds of Vermont, a rather colorless and undistinguished but uncompromisingly honest man, for the Republican nomination. He had managed to get the New York Republican convention to back Edmunds, but at the national convention in Chicago, the party chose Senator James G. Blaine of Maine as its candidate.

Blaine had great talent and charm, but his reputation for personal honesty had been blackened by a scandal involving some railroad bonds, and he was known to oppose the kind of reform to which Roosevelt was then committed. Many of Roosevelt's closest friends in politics refused to support Blaine, voting instead for the Democratic candidate, Grover Cleveland. Roosevelt, however, after deep soul searching, stood by Blaine, arguing that as a delegate to the convention he was duty bound to support the choice of the majority. This decision made his later career possible, for it convinced the Republican leadership that he was a loyal party man. But it cost him dearly among his personal friends, which depressed him deeply.

To find relief, he left his infant daughter with an aunt and went west to the cattle ranch he had purchased in the Dakota Badlands in 1883.

The story of Roosevelt the rancher is packed with excitement, adventure, and humor. The Dakota Territory was still raw frontier in the 1880's, and the arrival of a socialite New York dude was greeted by the hardened cowboys and the frontiersmen as an enormous joke. Roosevelt did not make things easier for himself by his appearance and manner. His idea of the proper cowboy costume included a broad sombrero-type hat, an elaborately fringed and beaded leather shirt, a braided bridle, and silver spurs. An expensive pearl-handled six-shooter hung from his hip. His thick glasses won him the nickname Four Eyes, while his refusal to drink, smoke, or swear convinced the tough locals that he was a sissy. On a roundup he called to his men, "Hasten forward quickly there!" and they almost fell from their saddles laughing.

But when they tried to bully this effete easterner, the cowboys were sadly disillusioned. Once, out hunting some lost horses, Roosevelt sought shelter on a cold night in the saloon of a strange town. A drunk was in the process of shooting up the face of the barroom clock. Seeing Roosevelt, the drunk flourished his guns and announced, "Four Eyes is going to treat." Ignoring the man, Roosevelt sat down by the stove to warm up, but the drunk came over, cursing vilely, and demanded that he buy the house a round of drinks. "Well," said Roosevelt, "if I've got to, I've got to," and rising from his chair, he struck the man on the jaw, knocking him cold.

Actions such as this soon convinced the ranching community that Roosevelt was neither a fool nor a coward. He also determinedly mastered the skills of the open range. On one occasion, when he was having difficulty mounting a half-wild bronco, a cowhand offered to help. "Cowboy," Roosevelt said, "I know you can ride him. What I want to find out is if I can ride him." Such behavior led one ranch foreman to comment: "That four-eyed maverick has got sand in his craw aplenty. He's sure a man to hold up his end."

Eventually, Roosevelt became a first-rate cowboy. An eyewitness gave an account of him as a broncobuster: "Roosevelt . . . had his grip, and like grim death he hung on. Hat, glasses, six-shooter, everything unanchored about him, took the count. But there was no breaking his grip. Like a burr, he stuck." By 1885 he had won a firm place in the ranching community. That year he helped organize the Little Missouri Stockmen's Association and was elected its chairman.

Although Roosevelt did not consider his ranch, which he named Elkhorn, primarily as a money-making venture, he worked as hard as any laborer. He spent weeks at a time in the saddle on roundups and endured the hardships of the open range cheerfully. One night, for example, Roosevelt was guarding a large herd when a sudden thunderstorm panicked the cattle, and they stampeded. All night long he galloped after them, finally heading the frightened beasts at dawn. After changing horses, he spent the entire next day hunting down strays. After forty hours in the saddle, he finally slept but rose at four the next morning for another full day's work.

Of course, Roosevelt was no ordinary cowhand. He did not live continuously on his ranch but returned to New York frequently to participate in his political activities. While at the ranch he found time to write a great deal: about ranch life, about the history of the West, about politics and hunting, even a biography of Thomas Hart Benton, a famous pre–Civil War senator from Missouri. He also indulged his passion for hunting to the full, penetrating the wildest regions in search of big game. On one hunt, he was set upon by five Indians, but he drove them off with his rifle. Another time he ranged as far west as Montana in search of the elusive mountain goat.

"Cocking my rifle and stepping quickly forward," he

wrote of an encounter with a bear in the rugged Big Horn Mountains, "I found myself face to face with the great bear, who was less than twenty-five feet off. . . . At that distance and in such a place it was very necessary to kill or disable him at the first fire; doubtless my face was pretty white, but the blue barrel was steady as a rock as I glanced along it until I could see the top of the bead fairly between his two sinister-looking eyes. As I pulled the trigger I jumped aside out of the smoke, to be ready if he charged, but it was needless, for the great brute was struggling in the death agony. . . . The bullet hole in his skull was exactly between his eyes. . . . This bear was nearly nine feet long and weighed over a thousand pounds."

Roosevelt could have made a political career for himself in the West, but his roots remained in New York despite his love of the ranching country. His second marriage, at the age of twenty-eight, in December, 1886, to Edith Kermit Carow, was another cause for settling down. Furthermore, the open-range cattle industry was struck by a series of natural disasters. The worst of these was the winter of 1886–87. Terrible blizzards, accompanied by temperatures of 40 to 50 degrees below zero, killed off about 75 percent of all the cattle on the plains. When Roosevelt, who had been honeymooning in Europe all that winter, returned to his ranch in April, he rode for three days across the land without seeing a live cow. In every ravine and valley he came upon dozens of rotting corpses. "We have had a perfect smashup all through the cattle country of the northwest," he wrote to his friend Congressman Henry Cabot Lodge of Massachusetts. "The losses are crippling. For the first time I have been utterly unable to enjoy a visit to my ranch. I shall be glad to get home." He did not dispose of his property until 1897, but after April, 1887, his ranching career was over.

He left behind a host of friends. "Theodore is a Dakota cowboy," the Sioux Falls *Press* recorded, paying him the region's highest compliment. "When he first went on the range, the cowboys took him for a dude, but . . . there is no man now who inspires such enthusiastic regard among them as he." As for Roosevelt, he summed up the impact of the West on himself on a visit in 1900. "Here the romance of my life began," he said. "Whatever may happen I can thank God I have lived and toiled with men."

CHAPTER 3

REFORMER

SHORTLY BEFORE HIS SECOND MARRIAGE, Roosevelt resumed his political career by running for mayor of New York on the Republican ticket. He did so reluctantly, for he knew he had little chance of being elected in the heavily Democratic city, especially in 1886. That year the Democrats had nominated an honest and highly regarded iron manufacturer, Abram S. Hewitt, for mayor. Furthermore, the reformer Henry George was seeking the office on the Union Labor ticket. George had written a famous book, *Progress and Poverty,* which argued that poverty could be abolished if all rents on land were taxed 100 percent. Naturally, this proposal alarmed property owners; fearful that George might be elected, many conservative Republicans in New York were prepared to vote for Hewitt. Roosevelt accepted the Republican nomination only out of a sense of duty to his party.

He campaigned hard, but his youth—he was still under thirty—counted against him, and to some conservatives he seemed almost as great a threat as Henry George. He ran a bad third on election day, attracting only 60,477 votes. Hewitt won with 90,466, while George received 67,930. The severity of this defeat discouraged Roosevelt greatly. He took to calling himself "a literary feller, not a politician," and indeed he devoted a great deal of his time for the next year or two to writing. Actually, he never thought seriously of giving up politics. In 1888 he campaigned for the Republican presidential candidate, Benjamin Harrison. When Harrison was elected, the young New Yorker was rewarded with an appointment to the United States Civil Service Commission.

For years reformers had been trying to abolish the

"spoils system," under which victorious politicians handed out government jobs to their followers, like pirates distributing booty. The appointments were usually made without much regard for the ability of the appointees to perform the duties of the offices. Every time a different party won control in Washington, its followers demanded jobs. To make places for them, competent workers had to be discharged in wholesale lots. This system decreased government efficiency and too often made office seeking a corrupt and bitter struggle. The assassination of President James A. Garfield in 1881, by a man who had failed to get a job, had aroused the public against the system. The next year, Congress passed a law placing some government offices outside the spoils system. To obtain these posts, candidates took examinations. Party affiliation was not considered. Once in office, they could not be removed so long as they performed their work properly. Congress also created a three-man Civil Service Commission to supervise the administration of this law and conduct the necessary examinations.

Like most Presidents of that era, Harrison had mixed

feelings about the civil service law. He found the demands of his followers for jobs time-consuming and annoying, but he realized that satisfying these demands strengthened his party's machine. In general, he sided with the politicians against the reformers; his Postmaster General, the department store magnate John Wanamaker, had soon fired 30,000 Democratic postmasters and replaced them with loyal Harrison men. Harrison appointed Roosevelt, an outspoken foe of the spoils system, in an attempt to quiet the protests of reformers that he was wrecking the civil service movement.

Roosevelt appeared to have little actual power as commissioner, but he soon proved that by using what power he had and by attracting the attention of the press, he could accomplish a great deal. From his first day as commissioner (when he burst into his office and snapped to a secretary, "I am the new Civil Service Commissioner. Have you a telephone? Call up the Ebbitt House. I have an engagement with Archbishop Ireland. Say I will be there at ten o'clock.") he dominated his two fellow commissioners. He issued attention-catching statements and reports and wrangled steadily with the politicians. More important, he enforced the civil service rules strictly, refusing to appoint candidates with powerful friends if they had not passed the examinations with high grades. He revised the tests for many jobs, making them more practical. For example, he made candidates for border guard demonstrate skills in shooting and riding, until, as one historian put it, the tests amounted to a kind of government-sponsored rodeo.

He battled steadily with Postmaster General Wanamaker, who, he said in a private letter, was like a pig, "oily, but with bristles sticking up through the oil." He became so exasperated with Harrison for his kowtowing to the spoilsmen that he called the President "a timid old psalm-singing Indianapolis politician." In 1891 Roosevelt discovered that the postmaster of Baltimore, with Wanamaker's approval, had dismissed about half the postal employees in his office, who were supposedly under the protection of the civil service law. When Wanamaker and Harrison refused to take action, Roosevelt demanded a congressional investigation. During this investigation, which revealed the accuracy of Roosevelt's charges, he openly called Wanamaker a liar. The incident hurt the Harrison administration and the Republican party, but when Roosevelt was convinced that a certain action was right, he never hesitated. Public interest in and support of civil service reform increased rapidly. Although President Harrison was furious, he did not dare remove the popular Roosevelt from office.

Harrison was defeated by Grover Cleveland in the 1892 presidential election in part at least because of his civil service policy. Cleveland kept Roosevelt on the commission and gave him far more support than Harrison had. When Roosevelt finally resigned in 1895, the number of civil service employees was more than twice as large as when he was first appointed. As one of his biographers, William H. Harbaugh, has written, Roosevelt's "imaginative and energetic enforcement of the laws had virtually institutionalized the civil service system."

Roosevelt gave up his civil service work to become police commissioner of New York City. A new reform mayor, William L. Strong, had just been elected, and he was eager to clean up the city's corrupt and inefficient police department. The force was indeed in bad shape. Patrolmen often got their jobs through political pull, and higher officers bought promotions openly—it was said that the job of captain could be had for $10,000. Police cooperated with gangsters, blinking at open violations of the law in return for bribes. Ordinary citizens complained of the surliness and inefficiency of the men in blue. Police methods were both antiquated and brutal.

Roosevelt tackled his new job with characteristic vigor. He sailed into headquarters in May, 1895, ready to conquer the world. The other three members of the police board promptly elected him president. Promising "to make matters very unpleasant for policemen who shirk their duty," he quickly won the backing of most of the newspapers, which thereafter gave his exploits reams of valuable publicity. Within ten days he had fired the operating head of the force, Superintendent Tom Byrnes. Soon Roosevelt was a familiar figure on the streets, popping up unexpectedly, day and night, at remote points, always on the lookout for improper police behavior. One time he came upon a policeman leaving a saloon with a glass of beer in his hand. Seeing the commissioner, the policeman threw the beer through the swinging doors and fled, but Roosevelt ran him down, grabbed him by the collar, took his number, and ordered him to appear for trial the next day. At night he often roamed the streets disguised in a black cloak and slouch hat, searching for policemen who were neglecting their duties. He also inspected the city's jails regularly. On one occasion he caught a woman prisoner pulling a string through her barred window. At the end of the string was a bottle of whiskey, evidently attached by a friend outside.

Besides these spectacular deeds, Roosevelt did a great deal to improve the morale and efficiency of the force. He was quick to reward heroism with promotion, and he did away almost completely with the use of political influence in obtaining appointments. "We paid not the slightest attention to a man's politics or creed, or where he was born. . . ." he later explained. He set up a board to examine applicants and established stiff physical standards too. The ideal policemen, he said, were "men of strong physique and resolute temper, sober, self-respecting, self-reliant, with a strong wish to improve themselves." He also modernized police methods. He created a bicycle squad (forerunner of the modern radio-car patrols), installed a telephone network to speed police communications, and improved the training of recruits.

"We have a real Police Commissioner," declared the New York *World*, singing the new commissioner's praises. "His teeth are big and white, his eyes are small and piercing, his voice is rasping. . . . His heart is full of reform, and a policeman in full uniform, with helmet, revolver and night stick is no more to him than a plain, every-day human being. . . ."

However, Roosevelt soon ran into serious trouble in his law-enforcement activities. There was on the statute books a state law prohibiting the sale of liquor on Sundays. To thousands of workingmen, especially those of German origin, this law seemed utterly unreasonable. On their one day of rest they demanded the right to visit a bar or beer garden for relaxation and companionship. As a result the Sunday-closing law was widely violated. Saloons remained officially closed, but patrons entered freely by side and back doors to get their drinks. This situation opened the way for much corruption. If a saloonkeeper paid off the police, he was not disturbed; if he did not, his place would be raided and closed up.

Although not a drinker himself, Roosevelt did not favor prohibition, on Sunday or any other day. Yet he recognized that the law was corrupting the police force, and he also believed that all laws, wise or foolish, should be impartially enforced. He therefore instructed the police to close all places where liquor was sold on the Sabbath. "I was only enforcing honestly a law that had hitherto been enforced dishonestly," he later explained. ". . . there was no protected class. Everybody was arrested alike. . . ."

This policy aroused a storm of protest—from liquor dealers, from crooked politicians, and from thousands of honest citizens deprived of their Sunday glass of beer. Undeterred, Roosevelt kept a tight lid on Sunday drinking, cracking down on posh restaurants and hotels as well as on the city's 12,000-odd neighborhood saloons. Soon even Mayor Strong was urging him to relent, but he refused to do so. Attempting to ease the conflict, the state legislature passed a new law authorizing the sale of liquor on Sundays with meals in hotels, a hotel being defined as any building containing ten bedrooms.

A host of fake hotels sprang up, some 2,000 in a few months. Most were low dives, catering to every vice. One "hotel" on the Bowery, for example, met the ten-bedroom rule merely by roofing over some horse stalls. A sign in this place read: "Sleeping In This Hotel Positively Prohibited." The new law made Roosevelt's job far more difficult. Formerly his men could close any place where liquor was being sold on Sunday; now they had to distinguish between legitimate hotels and false ones. Naturally, mistakes were made. Public protests mounted.

Gradually Roosevelt became discouraged; it was all very well to insist on enforcing the law but disheartening to act in a way that angered masses of decent citizens. His troubles were increased by a running conflict with one of his fellow commissioners, Andrew D. Parker. "It is very hard work indeed to go on with such a scoundrel," he complained. Mayor Strong finally removed Parker, but Roosevelt thought increasingly of resigning. When the Republican William McKinley was elected President in November, 1896, the possibility of a Federal job in the new administration attracted him strongly.

CHAPTER 4

ROUGH RIDER

IN THE SPRING OF 1897, PRESIDENT MCKINLEY offered to make him Assistant Secretary of the Navy, and Roosevelt accepted with pleasure.

Roosevelt had been interested in ships all his life and was an expert on naval history. He also came to the Navy Department at a crucial time: America, growing in wealth and population, stood on the verge of becoming a world power. As for the Navy itself, it had fallen from the high state of efficiency that Roosevelt had described in his first book, *The Naval War of 1812*. By the 1890's, however, its deficiencies were being rapidly corrected.

A new modern fleet of armored battleships and cruisers was taking shape.

Roosevelt's aggressive, patriotic nature put him in the forefront of those who, in the eighties and nineties, were advocating a powerful navy and an expansionist foreign policy. No doubt his long battle against fear and feebleness as a child led him to overstress the importance of bravery, power, and fighting. His rather naïve faith in his own ability to distinguish right from wrong with unfailing accuracy made him too willing to damn any foreign power whose policies conflicted with those of the United States. In any case, he was an extremist even among the most fervent advocates of what was called the large policy—a policy that called for military and territorial expansion even at the risk of war. He was a friend of Captain Alfred T. Mahan, whose famous studies of the influence of sea power affected him strongly.

Roosevelt at this point in his life was undoubtedly something of a warmonger. At various times he urged attacking Mexico, Germany, England, and Spain. In 1891 a trivial incident in Valparaiso, Chile, in which a group of

American sailors were arrested after a barroom brawl, led him to advocate war with Chile and to offer to raise a regiment for that purpose. He talked irresponsibly of seizing Canada, less drastically of annexing the Hawaiian Islands and other Pacific territory. He urged repeatedly that the United States build a canal across Central America, both for strategic purposes and to encourage foreign trade. As one congressman later said, "Roosevelt came down here [in 1897] looking for war. He did not care whom we fought as long as there was a scrap." This was not really an exaggeration. Roosevelt himself, in a letter that year, wrote to a friend, "In strict confidence, I should welcome any war. The country needs one."

Roosevelt's superior, Secretary of the Navy John D. Long, was an easygoing politician, content to allow his assistant to handle much of the routine work of the department. Soon, Roosevelt was busy visiting shipyards, revising naval regulations, urging Congress to build more battleships, and pushing forward talented young officers regardless of their length of service. Within days of his arrival in Washington, he was writing President

McKinley in great detail about the condition of various vessels: the "protected cruiser" *Philadelphia,* whose bottom needed scraping; the *Baltimore* and the *Charleston,* good cruisers undergoing necessary repairs; and the Navy's pride, the battleship *Oregon,* "an overmatch for half the entire Japanese navy."

He worked so hard because hard work was part of his nature, but also because he believed the nation would soon be at war with Spain over Cuba. That island, then a Spanish colony, was being torn by revolution. Brutal guerrilla warfare had led to harsh retaliation by the Spanish. Many Americans, already sympathetic to the Cubans' desire for independence, were outraged by newspaper reports, often exaggerated, of cruel Spanish treatment of Cuban civilians, including women and children. Roosevelt condemned Spain without restraint. "I cannot understand how the bulk of the people can tolerate the hideous infamy that has attended the last two years of Spanish rule in Cuba," he wrote early in 1898. "The time has come for us to fight."

President McKinley tried to maintain a scrupulous

neutrality in the Cuban revolution. Roosevelt disapproved of this, writing that McKinley had "no more backbone than a chocolate eclair." He was determined to prepare the Navy for instant action against Spain. John D. Long, following official policy, wished to proceed cautiously. But one day in February, 1898, when the secretary was away from Washington, Roosevelt boldly sent a cable to Commodore George Dewey, commander of the United States Asiatic fleet, based in Hong Kong. "Keep full of coal," he ordered. "In the event of declaration war . . . see that the Spanish squadron does not leave the Asiatic coast and then [begin] offensive operations in Philipine Islands." Of course, Long was angry when he discovered what Roosevelt had done. However, he did not countermand the order, and when war broke out in April, Dewey was ready. He promptly steamed to the Philippines and destroyed the Spanish fleet in Manila Bay, thus opening the way for American conquest of the islands.

Once war had been declared, Roosevelt could not be kept from the front lines. Against the urging of President McKinley and all his own friends that he remain at his desk in the Navy Department, and despite the fact that by this time he had a wife and six children to care for, he was determined to enlist. ". . . I have consistently preached the doctrine of a resolute foreign policy and of readiness to accept the arbitrament of the sword if necessary," he explained. "Now the occasion has arisen, and I ought to meet it. . . ." He resigned as Assistant Secretary of the Navy on May 6, 1898, announcing that he was organizing a volunteer cavalry regiment.

From all over the country, young men came forward to serve under him—cowboys and Indians, college boys, even some policemen who had worked with him in New York City. Since he lacked military training, Roosevelt contented himself with a commission as lieutenant colonel. His Rough Rider regiment was commanded by Colonel Leonard Wood, an experienced soldier who had won the Congressional Medal of Honor in the Indian wars.

The regiment trained at San Antonio, Texas, where the Rough Riders soon proved to be an undisciplined lot. Roosevelt did not help matters much, for he was too impetuous and warmhearted to be a stern officer. The men worshiped him. When he made a speech ordering them to stop "carousing" when on leave in San Antonio, they simply cheered. He did not improve the situation when after a hot training exercise he took the troop to an amusement park, ordered them to dismount, and then said, "The men can go in and drink all the beer they want, which I will pay for!" Fortunately Colonel Wood was a sound disciplinarian and soon molded the Rough Riders into an effective outfit.

Roosevelt fumed impatiently during the delay between the organization of the Rough Riders and their final disembarkation in Cuba. He tried to prepare for every eventuality, even buying a dozen pairs of steel-rimmed eyeglasses to make sure he would never be caught without one. He actually sewed several pairs into his campaign hat.

The regiment was finally moved to Tampa, Florida, where transports were waiting, but the camp there was utterly disorganized. Freight cars full of supplies were backed up for miles, and no one in authority seemed to know what was going on. "Each of us had to show an alert and not over-scrupulous self-reliance in order to obtain food for his men," he wrote.

Desperate to be aboard ship, Colonel Wood finally commandeered the transport *Yucatan*. But when Roosevelt prepared to march the men aboard, he discovered that a general had assigned the vessel to two other regiments. Glibly outtalking a senior officer, he hustled the Rough Riders on the ship, only to sweat disconsolately in torrid heat for nearly a week before the order to sail was given. Conditions on the packed *Yucatan* were "suggestive of the Black Hole of Calcutta," Roosevelt complained. When the sailing order was issued at last, on June 13, 1898, he was so happy that he performed "an impromptu war dance" before the troops. The Rough Riders were forced to leave their horses behind because of the shortage of space, but as Roosevelt said, "We would rather crawl on all fours than not go."

American strategy in the war with Spain called for landing at the eastern end of Cuba and attacking the port city of Santiago, where the Spanish Atlantic fleet had taken refuge. The Rough Riders went ashore at the village of Daiquiri on June 22. Two days later, at Las Guásimas, they saw their first action, losing sixteen men in a sharp skirmish. When Wood was promoted to brigadier general, Roosevelt took command of the regiment, becoming a full colonel on June 30. On July 1 Roosevelt was ordered to attack Kettle Hill, part of the San Juan highlands overlooking Santiago.

This was his "crowded hour," the greatest moment of his life, if not the most important. "I waved my hat," he wrote later, "and we went up the hill with a rush." Exposing himself recklessly, he led the Rough Riders' charge. Men fell all about him; he was grazed by a Spanish bullet; with his own gun he "doubled up a Spanish officer like a jack rabbit" as the man fled from a blockhouse. The Rough Riders carried Kettle Hill by nightfall and pushed on. But for several days thereafter, heavy Spanish counterattacks threatened their position.

"Charging these entrenchments against modern rifles is terrible," Roosevelt wrote from the battlefield. "For three days I have been at the extreme front of the firing line; how I have escaped I know not; I have not blanket or coat; I have not taken off my shoes even; I sleep in the drenching rain and drink putrid water." The men ate captured Spanish rations and slept in trenches, sniped at from the rear by enemy sharpshooters in trees. Almost 100 of Roosevelt's 490 men were killed or wounded.

At last the heights were cleared of Spaniards. With American artillery threatening the harbor of Santiago, the Spanish fleet had to put out to sea, where it was quickly destroyed by blockading American warships. Santiago surrendered, and within a matter of weeks the war was over. On August 15 the Rough Riders arrived back in the United States, their colonel a national hero.

No one admired what he had done more than Roosevelt himself, for he possessed a strong streak of egotism. His book about the campaign, called *The Rough Riders*, was so full of his own exploits that one reviewer, the humorist Finley Peter Dunne, suggested he should have called it "Alone in Cuba." Fortunately, the hero could also laugh at himself. When he read the review, he wrote a friendly letter to Dunne urging him to pay a visit. "I regret to state," he said, "that my family and intimate friends are delighted with your review." And along with the self-glorification, Roosevelt paid full tribute to the men he had led. When they presented him with a memento after their return home, he spoke movingly of his pride in them. For the rest of his life, he was continually finding jobs for or otherwise aiding former Rough Riders.

Undoubtedly a man of Roosevelt's intelligence, ambition, energy, and colorful personality would have had an important political career in any case, but his exploits in Cuba speeded his advance enormously. Before 1898 he had held no elective office higher than state assemblyman. Now, little more than a month after he had set foot again on American soil, he was nominated as the Republican candidate for governor of New York.

CHAPTER 5

GOVERNOR OF NEW YORK

AMERICAN MILITARY HEROES, STARTING WITH George Washington, have often done well in politics. Andrew Jackson's political career was made possible by his victory over the British at New Orleans in the War of 1812; Zachary Taylor's by his success in the Mexican War; U. S. Grant's by his defeat of the Confederacy in the Civil War; Dwight D. Eisenhower's by his leadership of the great Allied coalition that defeated Germany and Japan in World War II. Yet military heroes do not always go on to win public office. America's World War I commander General John J. Pershing never did, nor did Douglas MacArthur, hero of the Pacific fighting in World War II.

George Dewey, who crushed the Spanish fleet at Manila Bay, was a greater national hero than Roosevelt in 1898, but he could never turn his popularity to political advantage.

Of course, Theodore Roosevelt's amazing rise after 1898 did not depend entirely upon his fame as a Rough Rider. That fame made him, as the politicians say, "available." Other qualities enabled him to seize the opportunity. Actually, most professional Republican politicos distrusted Roosevelt. He was too independent-minded and antimachine for their tastes. They nominated him for governor only reluctantly and because he played his cards carefully.

The most important man in New York Republican politics after the Spanish-American War was United States Senator Thomas C. Platt. Platt had close connections with powerful business corporations and a host of friends among the minor politicians of the state. He was called the Easy Boss because he ruled by compromise and consultation rather than by domineering over his supporters. This quality made him leery of Roosevelt, who had tended in the past to act like the proverbial bull in the china shop when he wanted to get something accomplished quickly.

In 1898, however, Platt's political machine was in serious trouble because of scandals involving the regulation of life insurance companies and the operation of the state-owned Erie Canal. The Republicans needed a popular and thoroughly respectable man to head the state ticket, a role Roosevelt could obviously fill. One of Platt's associates, the railroad executive Chauncey M. Depew, rather cynically stated the advantages of a Roosevelt candidacy. If a heckler should ever try to embarrass a Republican speaker by bringing up the scandals, the orator could reply, "I am mighty glad you asked that question. We have nominated for governor a man who has demonstrated that he is a fighter for the right. . . . If he is elected . . . every thief will be caught and punished. . . ." Platt agreed with Depew that this made a good deal of sense. Yet, as he confided to a friend, he was afraid that Roosevelt's "impulsive nature" might lead him, once elected, to "fight those who put him in office."

He also insisted that Roosevelt refuse to accept an independent reform-party nomination, which some of Platt's own enemies were suggesting as a way of breaking the machine's power.

Roosevelt wanted very much to be governor, and his behavior showed that he had by this time learned to control his impetuosity; in fact, he had become an extremely shrewd politician. When Platt's lieutenant, Lemuel Quigg of New York City, frankly explained the Boss's doubts to the prospective candidate, Roosevelt replied, "I should not make war on Mr. Platt or anybody else if war could be avoided . . . I certainly would confer with the organization. . . . I would do so in the sincere hope that there might always result harmony of opinion and purpose." Although he added that in the last analysis he would have to depend upon his own judgment of what was right and good for the whole state, this promise to cooperate was enough to satisfy Platt. The New York senator announced to the press that he favored the Rough Rider for governor. After that, Roosevelt's nomination by the Republican state convention was merely routine.

In this, his first major effort to win voter support, Roosevelt showed true brilliance as a campaigner. Dressed in civilian clothes but wearing a broad-brimmed black felt hat reminiscent of Rough Rider garb, and accompanied by a group of Rough Riders in full uniform, he stormed across the state in a special train. He made dozens of hard-hitting speeches. He spoke on many topics, including the need to support President McKinley and an expansionist foreign policy, and the importance of honest government. However, as one Republican leader put it, ". . . the speech was nothing, but the man's presence was everything, it was electrical, magnetic. . . . I looked in the faces of hundreds and saw only pleasure and satisfaction."

Roosevelt made few promises and advanced no detailed plans. His personality, which radiated bluff honesty, energy, and a refreshing unconventionality, was enough. Once, one of his crude Rough Rider supporters made an impromptu speech from the back of the campaign train. Colonel Roosevelt, he said, "kept ev'y promise he made to us and he will to you. He told us we might meet wounds and death and we done it, but he was thar in the midst of us, and when it came to the great day he led us up San Juan Hill like sheep to the slaughter and so he will lead you." Even this horrendous mistake made no difference—the crowd cheered. On election day in November, 1898, Roosevelt carried the state by 17,794 votes against the Democratic candidate, Augustus Van Wyck. The margin was close only because the tide was running toward the Democrats; without Roosevelt the Republicans would probably have been badly defeated.

Boss Platt had hesitated to back Roosevelt partly because he had genuine doubts about the Rough Rider's capacity for responsible leadership. "If he becomes governor of New York," Platt told Quigg, "sooner or later, with his personality, he will have to be a candidate for President of the United States." The two years of Roosevelt's governorship gave Platt ample opportunity to judge whether his fears had been justified. When the term ended, Platt was far from pleased with Roosevelt, but the governor had demonstrated both soundness and moderation. He had also worked out the basic ideas and techniques that he would employ when the lightning struck and he found himself in the White House.

Roosevelt's way of running the state quickly captured the public's attention. Each morning he would walk briskly to his office at the state capitol, scrambling up the broad stairs two at a time instead of taking the elevator. He conducted official business efficiently and on schedule; specific times were set aside for answering mail, consulting advisers, and meeting with reporters. Roosevelt got on exceptionally well with the newsmen. Of course, he was "good copy" to begin with, but they liked him also because he was always available and always frank. Instead of saying "no comment" when asked about something he did not want to discuss for political reasons, he would often answer off the record. This meant that although he held the reporters honor bound not to print his statement, he was still willing that they, as insiders, should be told what was going on.

He dealt with the touchy question of his relations with Boss Platt quite straightforwardly. His reformer friends wanted him to have nothing to do with Platt. To have followed their advice would have attracted headlines and would have been popular with the man in the street, but it would probably not have led to constructive legislation. Platt's machine was too strongly entrenched in the state legislature to be smashed by direct attack. Instead, Roosevelt made every possible effort to persuade Platt to go along with his plans. First of all, he consulted with the Boss openly and treated him with politeness and respect at all times. Instead of adopting a holier-than-thou attitude, he tried to convince Platt that the public interest required certain reforms. If change was resisted, he argued, radicals would push through more drastic measures than he was advocating.

In this way he persuaded Platt to agree to a number of significant liberal reforms, including even a new state civil service law that struck at the heart of the machine's power—the ability to hand out jobs to its followers. In cases where this method failed, the governor would decide that "the time had come when I had to show my teeth a little." Then he would talk ominously of still more radical changes, or draw upon his influence with powerful newspapers, or appeal over Platt's head to the younger, more independent members of the legislature. "If you choose to be cattle, I must consult your driver," he told two members of the assembly on one occasion. "Be men and I want your advice." Since in nearly every instance Roosevelt was seeking only moderate reforms, and since he usually was willing to accept less than he originally had asked for as long as some progress was made, these methods paid off.

Thus, the most interesting thing about Roosevelt's governorship is the light it throws on his essentially middle-of-the-road position, which seems out of keeping with his self-righteous, aggressive character. Although he tended personally to draw sharp distinctions between right and wrong, he was a political pragmatist: one who deals with things as they are and who avoids taking an all-out stand for desirable but unattainable objectives. Time after time in New York he acted as a balance wheel between the reformers and the conservatives. He advocated gradual change. He realized that the reformers were correct in arguing that the enormous industrial growth of the United States necessitated the passage of new laws, even the development of new philosophies of government. But he also knew that it was dangerous to try to remodel the complicated machinery of government too rapidly, and impossible to alter men's basic ideas overnight.

One area where Roosevelt's moderation appeared most clearly was that involving state regulation of large corporations. Big businesses had frequent dealings with the state government. They obtained many favors and advantages from laws, and conferred many benefits on the public, both in the goods and services they produced and in the taxes they paid. Many citizens, while appreciating the benefits gained, resented the wealth and power of the corporations. Some even felt that they were a threat to democratic government. Roosevelt took the position that the rights of both the big businessmen and the public must be protected; he stood for fair and equal treatment of each.

The question became critical in 1899. At issue was a new proposal placing a tax on corporation franchises.

These franchises were special charters giving particular companies the sole right to carry on their business in a specified area. Railroads, streetcar lines, electric-light companies, and other public utilities had to obtain them to do business. Once obtained, however, a franchise protected the holder against competition by rival companies. Corporations with franchises paid the regular state taxes on their real estate and other property, but until 1899, they did not pay taxes upon the franchises themselves, which of course were enormously valuable.

In that year State Senator John Ford of New York City introduced a bill taxing franchises. Boss Platt opposed it, while most reform groups supported it strongly. Roosevelt, trying to avoid a clash, first suggested delay until a legislative committee could investigate the franchise tax question carefully. But mounting public support for the idea convinced him that some kind of franchise tax ought to be levied promptly. The state senate then passed the Ford bill by a large majority. Roosevelt felt that this particular bill was too drastic, and he hoped the assembly would modify it. But when Platt's friends in the assembly tried to block any bill at all, he became irritated. Next, various corporation leaders threatened to cut off all campaign contributions in future elections if the law was passed. Furious, the governor demanded that the assembly pass the senate bill as it was. Under this pressure, the assembly gave in, and the bill was sent to Roosevelt for his signature.

At this point, Roosevelt displayed his political skill. Holding the radical bill over the heads of the conservatives, he delayed signing it. He demanded that the legislature, which had adjourned, reassemble in special session and pass amendments taking some of the sting out of the law. By then, even Boss Platt was ready to do what Roosevelt wished. Platt's henchmen in the legislature meekly submitted, and the final franchise tax law closely followed the governor's desires. Thus, Roosevelt was able both to defeat the machine and the business interests and to make them give their approval to his actions.

The public at large, mostly unconcerned with the exact form of the franchise tax, drew a clear conclusion from the controversy: their governor placed the general interest first; he would yield neither to extreme radicals nor to extreme conservatives. Roosevelt expressed this attitude well in a letter to Platt. ". . . we Republicans," he wrote, "set our faces as resolutely against improper corporate influence on the one hand as against demagogy and mob rule on the other."

Roosevelt applied the same philosophy to labor problems. He supported schemes to improve the lot of workingmen but stood fast against any attempt by workers to attain their goals by force. He had not forgotten the dreadful conditions he had seen in the tenement sweatshops while he was still a member of the state legislature. But a law forbidding the manufacture of cigars in tenements had been declared unconstitutional by the state court of appeals—a decision Roosevelt later characterized as "one of the most serious setbacks which the cause of industrial and social progress and reform ever received."

As governor, he therefore pushed through a new law requiring state inspection and licensing of all tenements in which manufacturing was taking place. He supported the demands of schoolteachers for higher salaries and engineered a measure strengthening the eight-hour-day law for all state employees. He fought unsuccessfully for a law insuring workers against accidents in certain dangerous businesses. More important, though less attention catching, was his constant effort to make sure that the state factory inspectors performed all their duties honestly and industriously.

But when streetcar employees in Brooklyn went on strike, he suggested the use of local militia to keep the cars running, even though most impartial observers agreed that the demands of the workers were justified. In another dispute involving construction workers on a dam in Westchester County, he actually did use the state militia. "No disorder must be permitted," he announced. Nevertheless, he was not antilabor, considering the standards of the day. He ordered an investigation to make sure that the employers had not violated the state eight-hour-day law in this dispute and expressed the personal opinion that the workers' wages were "too low."

"I think I have been the best Governor [of New York]

within my time," Roosevelt said in 1900. While they might disapprove of his boasting, most historians would agree with this judgment. In a difficult period, the state, under his direction, made significant progress toward adjusting to the needs of an industrial society.

CHAPTER 6

RELUCTANT VICE-PRESIDENT

AS GOVERNOR OF NEW YORK ROOSEVELT HAD profited personally, not merely by winning a national reputation but by gaining valuable experience in running a complicated governmental organization. He had learned how to deal with the conflicting demands of different political and economic forces in a democratic system. Most important of all, he was rapidly developing a new, modern conception of the role of the head of a state (or of a nation) as a representative of the common interest of the whole community. "He has torn down the curtain that shut in the governor," the *New York Times* recorded, "and taken the people into his confidence . . . beyond what was ever known before."

Roosevelt had not, however, won the confidence either of professional politicians like Platt or of the business leaders of the country. He was eager to run for a second term as governor in 1900. Boss Platt, dead-set against this, knew he could not prevent the popular governor's renomination directly. Instead, he sought to "elevate him to a higher position" in order to get him out of New York. That "higher position" was the Vice-Presidency. In 1900 President McKinley would be running for his second term, but since Vice-President Garret A. Hobart had died in 1899, he would have to find a new running mate. The popular, energetic Roosevelt seemed to Platt the perfect choice.

The Boss broached the subject to Roosevelt in January, 1900. Roosevelt hesitated. Of course the office would be a great honor, and there was always the chance that McKinley might die, thus opening the door of the White House. However, aside from his desire to continue his work as governor for two more years, he felt that the

Vice-Presidency was too inactive a post for a man of his restless energies. Overshadowed by McKinley, as Vice-President he would have mainly ceremonial duties.

The idea of having to preside over the Senate particularly distressed Roosevelt. "I am a comparatively young man . . . and I like to work," he explained to his friend Lodge, who was urging him to accept Platt's suggestion. "I do not like to be a figurehead. It would not entertain me to preside in the Senate . . . I could not do anything." When Lodge, Platt, and many other politicians, some genuine friends, others really trying to put him on the shelf, continued to press him to seek the nomination, he twisted and turned in an almost comical effort to avoid doing so. He would be willing to serve McKinley as Secretary of War or as civilian governor of the newly acquired Philippine Islands, he said. "I would greatly rather be anything, say a professor of history, than Vice-President," he claimed.

At first, rather naïvely, he had thought Platt's suggestion was based on friendship. "I believe Platt rather likes me, though I render him uncomfortable by some of the things I do," he said after the Boss first asked him to run. Then, as the truth dawned, he decided that "the big-monied men with whom he is in close touch," especially "the great corporations affected by the franchise tax," were behind Platt's attempt to get him out of New York. For a time, knowledge of Platt's motive made him more determined than ever to avoid the higher office. He announced that he would retire to private life rather than run for Vice-President. He even traveled to Washington to tell President McKinley that he firmly intended to continue as governor.

The situation was complicated by the fact that the single most powerful figure in Republican national politics, Senator Mark Hanna of Ohio, did not want Roosevelt as Vice-President. Hanna had great influence with McKinley, for he was a close personal friend and had played a large role in engineering the nomination and election of his fellow Ohioan as President four years earlier. Hanna's opinion of Roosevelt was similar to Platt's, but he lacked Platt's selfish motive for wanting to get the governor out of New York. He did not wish to put the headstrong, "unreliable" former Rough Rider in a position in which, as he said, "only one life" would stand between him and the Presidency.

Of course, if McKinley did not desire to have Roosevelt as his running mate, no power on earth could get him the nomination. McKinley, however, would not rule out Roosevelt or anyone else. He was determined, he said, to leave the choice of the vice-presidential candidate to the delegates who would gather at the Republican convention in Philadelphia in June.

Perhaps the President was being shrewd rather than weak or indecisive. He was certainly a very clever politician. (The reporter William Allen White once said that McKinley kept his ear so close to the ground to catch the rumblings of public opinion that a grasshopper could jump into it.) He did not want to offend his friend Senator Hanna, but he surely realized that Roosevelt would make a strong candidate.

The New Yorker's energy and impulsiveness, McKinley must have reasoned, would provide a nice balance to his own serene, rather passive nature. Roosevelt was a proven stump speaker, whereas McKinley preferred to remain at his home at Canton, Ohio, during election contests, conducting what was known as a front-porch campaign. Furthermore, as the hero of the Spanish-American War, Roosevelt had an enormous following among veterans and other patriotic groups. His support of the administration's expansionist foreign policy would help in a contest against the probable Democratic presidential candidate, William Jennings Bryan, who was likely to attack McKinley for having annexed the Philippine Islands after the war. Roosevelt also had a wide geographical appeal. As a successful governor of the most populous state in the Union, he would help secure New York and perhaps other eastern states for the Republicans. Yet westerners also loved the former cowboy-rancher. With McKinley strong in the Middle West and among conservative businessmen, a McKinley-Roosevelt ticket seemed unbeatable.

All these factors played into Platt's hands. Naturally, Roosevelt could have prevented his own nomination if he had stuck to his guns. But if he had, he might have ruined his career. For one so young to reject the Vice-Presidency as beneath him would have seemed presumptuous indeed. Platt was correct when he said after his arrival in Philadelphia in June, "Roosevelt might as well stand under Niagara Falls and try to spit water back as to stop his nomination. . . ."

The two had a last showdown on June 19 in a Philadelphia hotel room. Platt threatened to block Roosevelt's nomination for governor if he refused the Vice-Presidency. Roosevelt shot back angrily that he was ready for "a straight-out fight." However, in the end he gave in, not for fear of Platt, but in the realization that he would hurt himself by refusing. The convention nominated him almost unanimously. "I am completely reconciled," he admitted, "I believe it all for the best. . . . I should be a conceited fool if I was discontented with the nomination when it came in such a fashion."

Roosevelt then plunged into the contest against the Democrats with characteristic vigor. Mark Hanna, again managing the campaign, now made the best of the situation and relied heavily on the former Rough Rider.

Roosevelt "will be the star attraction of the performance," Hanna told reporters. When Roosevelt suggested that it might be undignified for a governor to make speeches outside his home state, Hanna told him that if he was worried about his dignity he should dress more conservatively, get rid of his Rough Rider hat, and try not to shout so loudly when he spoke.

Roosevelt responded manfully. He toured all over the country, making hundreds of speeches to more than three million people. "Teddy . . . ain't r-runnin'," the humorist Finley Peter Dunne wrote, "he's gallopin'." He spoke, as candidates usually do, rather vaguely about the variety of issues. He defended overseas expansion and struck out at monopolistic corporations, reactionary businessmen, and other "unhealthy, destructive, and antisocial elements" without specifying exactly how he thought such villains should be handled. On election day the McKinley-Roosevelt ticket won an impressive victory over Bryan and his running mate, Adlai E. Stevenson of Illinois. The margin in the popular vote was more than 850,000, the largest in a generation.

Never one for playing down his own accomplishments, Roosevelt wrote after the election: "Aside from McKinley and Hanna, I feel that I did as much as anyone in bringing about the result." Although McKinley would probably have been elected no matter who his running mate had been, this statement was a fair estimate of Roosevelt's contribution. In any case, he was now Vice-President of the United States and only forty-two years old.

CHAPTER 7

YOUNGEST MAN IN THE WHITE HOUSE

THE MIGHT-HAVE-BEENS OF HISTORY ARE fascinating, although impossible to untangle. By 1900 Theodore Roosevelt had his sights set on becoming President. He was too sensible to pursue the goal directly. When friends suggested that he run for Vice-President because the office would be a stepping-stone to the White House, he said, "To consider the Presidency in any way as a possibility would be foolish. . . . The only thing for me to do is to do exactly as I have always done; and that is, when there is a chance of attempting a bit of work worth the trial, to attempt it."

He had argued against running for Vice-President because he thought he would be "planted" for four years, unable to perform any "work worth the trial." But he was wrong. As early as Inauguration Day, March 4, 1901, when he took the oath as Vice-President, prominent newspapers were speculating about his chances of taking the presidential oath on the next Inauguration Day.

He had also worried about becoming bored with his official duties as Vice-President. Fortunately he did not have to spend much time presiding over the Senate, which met for only a few days after the inauguration to approve McKinley's major appointments before adjourning until December, 1901.

Thereafter, Roosevelt spent very little time in Washington. He busied himself with plans for resuming his study of the law, made speeches before such varied organizations as the Long Island Bible Society and the Fish and Game League, conducted a seminar for Harvard and Yale undergraduates at Sagamore Hill, his house at Oyster Bay, Long Island. The Vice-President even planned to hunt grizzly bears and wolves in Colorado, dreaming that "we could kill a big grizzly or silver-tip with our knives, which would be great sport."

Occasionally he fretted about his lack of authority and responsibility. "The Vice-Presidency . . . ought to be abolished," he told his old commander, General Leonard Wood. "I do not think that the President wants me to take any part in affairs, or give him any advice." Nevertheless, he kept himself fully occupied.

Then, on September 6, 1901, a madman named Leon Czolgosz shot William McKinley as the President reached out to shake his hand during a reception at the Pan-American Exposition in Buffalo. Roosevelt, who had been making a speech in upstate New York, hastened to the scene. Whatever his ambitions, he was genuinely shocked and full of concern for his chief. However, McKinley's wound did not seem serious. Roosevelt remained in Buffalo for a few days, but his letters show that he expected the President to make a quick recovery. On September 10, partly to show the country that McKinley was in no danger, he left to join his family at a lodge in the Adirondack Mountains.

On September 12, however, McKinley took a sudden, final turn for the worse. The next afternoon a messenger reached Roosevelt on the slopes of Mt. Tahawus with the news. Again he left for Buffalo, but during the early hours of September 14, while Roosevelt was hurrying toward a railroad station in upstate New York, McKinley died. Theodore Roosevelt, forty-two years old, had become the youngest President in the history of the United States.

What sort of a President would this headstrong, colorful young man make? Opinions differed. In general, the man in the street looked forward to new, exciting developments. Roosevelt was, above all, interesting; people waited expectantly to see what he would do. Many business leaders and conservative politicians had their doubts. It was not that they thought Roosevelt was a radical. Rather, they feared he would act impulsively, without proper consideration for the heavy responsibilities of his office. His frequently warlike statements and his sometimes uncontrolled criticisms of big business frightened them. His brother-in-law Douglas Robinson told him, "There is a feeling in financial circles that . . .

you may change matters so as to upset the confidence of the business world. . . ."

Mark Hanna, whose worries were increased by his genuine sorrow at the death of his close friend McKinley, is supposed to have exploded, "That damned cowboy is President of the United States!" When Roosevelt wrote him after taking the oath of office to suggest a meeting, Hanna replied, "Go slow . . . reserve decision" on all important questions. Actually, there was no chance that Roosevelt would go off half-cocked. His first act as President was to announce that "it shall be my aim to continue absolutely unbroken the policy of President McKinley. . . ." And for months he followed Hanna's advice to "go slow."

For this there were many reasons. Knowing that a number of persons of great influence considered him unreliable, he worked to allay their doubts. He was also, naturally enough, somewhat shaken by the awful event that had projected him so suddenly to the highest office in the land. "It is a dreadful thing to come into the Presidency in this way," he wrote. Roosevelt needed time to get his bearings. He had to learn the routine of life in the White House and absorb the thousands of details necessary for the performance of his duties.

Furthermore, any sudden attempt to put forward new legislation was likely to fail. Congress was firmly controlled by conservatives like Hanna and Platt, men suspicious of his views and resentful because they realized that their own actions had made possible his rise to power. Finally, from his first day as President, Roosevelt was determined to win re-election in his own right in 1904. He was therefore eager not to make enemies, especially before he knew exactly what he wanted to accomplish.

On the other hand, a man with his personality could not sit idle for long or let others lead when power lay in his hands. At home and abroad the country was entering a new phase in its history. The marvelous economic growth of the post-Civil War years had produced immense wealth, and the Spanish-American War had demonstrated that the United States was a world power. The men who feared Roosevelt were those who had produced, and who still controlled, this wealth. Most of them, perhaps understandably, wanted to keep things as they were. But along with new wealth and power had come new national problems: slums and sweatshops; corruption of government by powerful economic interests; a large increase in industrial accidents caused by high-speed machinery; the wasteful use of natural resources; a great and growing gap between rich and poor, especially between the masses of industrial workers and the handful of millionaire businessmen who employed them.

In foreign affairs, America had emerged from the war with Spain with colonies scattered from Puerto Rico to the Philippines. Latin America, especially the lands surrounding the Caribbean Sea, loomed large in the nation's thinking. This area was important for reasons of national defense, as a source of raw materials, and as a market for American manufactured goods. It was also going to be necessary to play a larger role in world politics, to pay close attention to the actions of the great European powers. The old days of splendid isolation from the rest of the world were over, although millions of Americans still refused to face the fact.

Roosevelt sensed these trends better than most, even if he was not always sure what should be done about them. He was certain, however, that if he did not act, others would. In many states new leaders were emerging (men like Robert M. LaFollette, governor of Wisconsin; George Norris, representative from Nebraska; and Albert J. Beveridge, senator from Indiana) who were calling themselves progressives. They were far from radical, but they were aware that industrialism and overseas expansion had produced problems as well as advantages, and they wanted to do something about it. They had great faith in the intelligence and goodness of the average man, and they believed that the economic and social evils of the times were caused by a breakdown of communication between the people and their government. If the government could be made to reflect the will of the majority rather than that of a few professional politicians and a clique of rich men, solutions to the problems of the day that were fair to all could easily be worked out.

Such a truly democratic government could safely be entrusted with much power; it could then attack current problems and eliminate them. Poverty, bad working conditions, and similar evils would be removed. Yet a progressive government would not destroy the legitimate rights and privileges of the wealthy. Once in power, the people would deal with such persons justly. For example, progressives were alarmed about the growth of trusts, which were combinations of large corporations created to monopolize particular industries. Progressives wanted either to break up the trusts and make the separate companies compete with one another or closely regulate their activities by law. However, they did not seek the socialization (government ownership) of industry. Nor did they want to destroy wealth or hamper the activities of legitimate businessmen in any way. They were moderate, middle-class reformers, as convinced as any of the conservatives of the sacredness of private property and individual freedom but eager to see these things made available to everybody.

Roosevelt was by no means an advanced progressive.

His support of reform was heavily influenced by his admiration of things as they were; he argued for moderate change as the best defense against drastic change, and in this sense he was more a conservative than a progressive. He knew that men like Senator Hanna and Representative Joseph G. Cannon of Illinois, whose slogan was "stand pat," were trying to hold back the tide of history—a hopeless task. If they had their way, he believed, the pressure for change would simply build up explosive force, endangering the entire private-enterprise system.

He proceeded cautiously, consulting conservative Republican leaders at every step. His first annual message in December, 1901, was full of reassurances to businessmen. His early requests for new legislation were confined to such noncontroversial matters as the construction of irrigation dams. Roosevelt steered clear of touchy questions like the protective tariff on manufactured products, which many reformers felt was fostering monopolies by keeping lower-priced foreign goods out of the country, and currency and banking reform, which had caused political divisions in the past.

Just the same, he was rapidly changing things simply by the way he was running the government. No President had ever been more eager to know what was going on all over the country, to discover what people were thinking and feeling. Streams of visitors poured in and out of his office, not only politicians and businessmen but writers, labor leaders, social workers, scientists, sports figures, and many others. He read omnivorously and with incredible speed, sending for dozens of books from the Library of Congress and going through newspapers and magazines by the hundreds. "Now and then I am asked as to 'what books a statesman should read,' " he wrote in 1913. "My answer is poetry and novels [and also] interesting books on history and government, and books of science and philosophy. . . ." He went on and on in his enthusiasm for books of all kinds.

But Roosevelt led an active, vigorous life despite his reading and the load of paper work he had to cope with. Whenever possible he combined business with exercise and recreation. When he wanted to discuss future legislation with a congressman, or foreign relations with a diplomat, he would frequently invite the man to go horseback riding with him, or play tennis, or hike in Rock Creek Park. Senator Beveridge, a rising leader among the Republican progressives, was soon joking that anyone who wanted to have influence in Washington would have to buy a horse. Roosevelt himself, aware of this kind of talk, quipped that his friend Senator Lodge, actually an excellent rider, "was frantic with fury when they said he was learning to ride, so as to go out with me." Washington insiders were soon gossiping about the President's "tennis cabinet," a group of close friends with whom he discussed policy while dashing about the court. And humorists and cartoonists poked fun at the poor, fat, sweating diplomats and other dignitaries who puffed after the indefatigable "T.R." as he plunged through brush and briar on his famous hikes.

Yet Roosevelt's exuberance and informality did not interfere with his efficiency as an administrator. He disliked red tape but knew how necessary it was to deal with routine business in an orderly way. He loved his friends dearly but never let personal feelings interfere with government business. He played no favorites, he gave no crony a job beyond the man's talents. Every branch of the government came beneath his watchful eye, for he loved to exercise power. But he was also willing to take advice, delegate authority, and trust subordinates to do their jobs without constant checking. The job of being President, he wrote after a little more than a year in office, "is one long strain on the temper . . . one long experiment of checking one's impulses with an iron hand and learning to subordinate one's own desires to what some hundreds of associates can be forced or cajoled or led into desiring."

Although he did not try to persuade Congress to pass many progressive laws, Roosevelt accomplished a good deal by his inspired use of his position as chief representative of all the people and by his skillful use of the government departments under his control. In May, 1902, 50,000 anthracite coal miners of Pennsylvania went on strike for higher wages, an eight-hour day, and recognition of their union. The mine owners refused even to discuss terms with the union, however, and the strike dragged on through the summer. Coal prices rose sharply, and as winter approached, the threat of a serious shortage caused great alarm. Most people sympathized with the workers, especially after they agreed to submit their case to the decision of impartial arbitrators. Even Mark Hanna believed that the miners deserved better conditions and that the owners were behaving unfairly.

Roosevelt had no power to force a settlement of the strike, but he decided that the national interest required action. He summoned both sides to a conference at the White House and asked them as loyal Americans to end the strike. Once again the workers' representatives agreed to outside arbitration, but the owners, furious at the President for having forced them to meet with the union, refused. They demanded that he use troops to end the strike. "The operators," Roosevelt later recalled, "came down in a most insolent frame of mind, refused to talk of arbitration or other accommodation of any kind, and used language that was insulting to the miners and offensive to me."

Instead of doing what the owners wished, he indicated

that unless they agreed to arbitration he would send troops into the area, not to break the strike but to seize and operate the mines in the public interest.

This forced the owners to terms. At another White House meeting they agreed to allow Roosevelt to appoint a commission to settle the dispute. He even got the owners to agree to the appointment of a union official to this commission—a man whom Roosevelt called an "eminent sociologist."

The public cheered the President. He had compelled powerful business interests to submit to the general will, but he had done so fairly, without imposing his own ideas about the actual terms. The incident also marked another important step in his own development as a progressive. "The labor problem in this country had entered upon a new phase," he later explained.

"All citizens who gave thought to the matter saw that the labor problem was not only an economic, but also a moral, a human problem. Individually the miners were impotent when they sought to enter a wage contract with the great companies; they could make fair terms only by uniting into trade-unions to bargain collectively. The men were forced to cooperate to secure not only their economic but their simple human rights. . . . A simple and poor society can exist as a democracy on a basis of sheer individualism. But a rich and complex industrial society cannot so exist. . . . No group of men may so exercise their rights as to deprive the nation of the things which are necessary and vital to the common life." These ideas, which seem so familiar today, had never before been expressed by a President of the United States.

Another dramatic example of Roosevelt's use of presidential power was his antitrust suit against the Northern Securities Company, a combination of western railroads. In 1890 Congress had passed a law, the Sherman Antitrust Act, which made it illegal for companies to combine in order to destroy or reduce competition. This law had been difficult to enforce because the Supreme Court had interpreted it very narrowly. By the time Roosevelt became President, it was practically a dead letter.

Roosevelt personally believed that the monopoly

problem should be solved by having the government regulate the trusts instead of breaking them up. Yet he knew that Congress was unwilling to pass laws controlling the activities of private businesses. That smacked of socialism, whereas the antitrust law was based on the principle of protecting free competition, which almost everyone in America supported wholeheartedly. Since Roosevelt's main object was to protect the public against the abuses of monopolistic corporations, he therefore decided to use the Sherman Antitrust Act even though he did not consider it an ideal weapon.

The fact that the Supreme Court had apparently made the law impossible to enforce did not stop him. Casting about for a monopoly to attack, he settled upon the Northern Securities Company. This organization made a perfect target. Its separate parts, the Northern Pacific, the Great Northern, and the Chicago, Burlington and Quincy railroads controlled nearly all the track between Chicago and the Pacific northwest. It was dominated by the mighty Wall Street banker J. P. Morgan, who was widely regarded as the master monopolist of the country and thus was disliked and distrusted by the man in the street. The creation of this monopoly had been accompanied by a stock-market panic and much bad publicity.

Early in 1902, the White House announced that the President had ordered his Attorney General, Philander C. Knox, to bring suit against the Northern Securities Company for violation of the Sherman Antitrust Act. Business leaders were indignant, accusing Roosevelt of disregarding previous Supreme Court decisions and threatening the entire capitalistic system. J. P. Morgan was especially upset, not merely because one of his companies was under attack but because the suit implied that he was a criminal. He believed that he was operating within the law; if the President thought otherwise, he should tell him so informally and give him a chance to set matters right. Hastening to Washington, he said to Roosevelt, "If we have done anything wrong, send your man to my man and they can fix it up." When Roosevelt replied tersely, "That can't be done," the banker asked him if he intended to attack his "other interests," meaning the gigantic United States Steel Corporation and a number of other trusts that Morgan controlled. Roosevelt assured him that if these companies violated the law they would be punished; if they did not, of course they could operate freely.

Two years after this confrontation took place, the Supreme Court finally decided that the Northern Securities Company was indeed violating the Sherman Antitrust Act. The Supreme Court thus reversed its earlier ruling. This enabled the government to proceed against other trusts. Roosevelt won from the affair another nickname, the Trust Buster. Although he did not really want to break up big combinations, the name was well deserved, for it implied that he was determined to make big businesses obey the law. Again, the experience with Morgan illustrated Roosevelt's belief that the President was guardian of the national interest. "Mr. Morgan could not help regarding me as a big rival operator," he noted. Roosevelt rejected this "Wall Street point of view" outright and did a great deal to educate the public to reject it also.

In his dealings with foreign nations, Roosevelt used

presidential power even more vigorously. Critics had been particularly worried that the belligerent Rough Rider would quickly involve the country in war. This, of course, did not happen; the responsibility of his office made him less aggressive. In his conduct of foreign policy, he revealed a realistic understanding of how nations deal with one another and an awareness that a powerful country like the United States had to participate actively in world affairs. He insisted that the only true security lay in strength; that a country without a strong armed force could not be safe from attack. "Don't bluster," he once said, "don't flourish a revolver, and never draw unless you intend to shoot."

American security, Roosevelt believed, depended upon having a powerful navy and full control over the waters surrounding the country. To guarantee this security, he sometimes disregarded the interests of the small republics of the Caribbean area, from Cuba to Colombia. His purpose in these actions was not to dominate these tiny neighbors or build an American empire. Rather he moved to protect the United States against possible attack by one of the great European naval powers, which might try to establish bases in the area if it was not checked by the United States.

His first objective was to build a canal across Central America so that the United States Navy could steam quickly from one ocean to the other in time of emergency. He also argued, along with many others, that a canal would have enormous commercial advantages. There were two possible routes for an interoceanic waterway, one in Nicaragua, the other across the Isthmus of Panama.

After considerable investigation, Roosevelt decided upon the Panama route, partly because it was shorter, partly because a private French company had already done some of the work. Panama was then a state in the Republic of Colombia. In 1903 Secretary of State John Hay negotiated a treaty with Colombia leasing a zone across Panama to the United States and giving it the right to construct and operate a canal. Colombia was to receive $10,000,000 in gold and an annual rent of $250,000. But the Colombian senate refused to ratify this treaty, holding out for a higher price.

There was some justice to the Colombian position, for the United States was prepared to pay the French canal company $40,000,000 for its assets, far more than Colombia had been offered. But Roosevelt was furious when the treaty was rejected. He said the Colombians were "mad to get hold of the forty million of the Frenchmen," and added, "You could no more make an agreement with the Colombian rulers than you could nail currant jelly to a wall." Instead of negotiating further or moving the project to Nicaragua, he seized the opportunity offered by the outbreak of a revolution in Panama on November 3, 1903, to snatch the zone. He sent a cruiser, the U.S.S. *Nashville,* to Panama to prevent Colombian forces from suppressing the revolution. Three days after the rebels had declared their independence, Roosevelt recognized the new government, and two weeks later, he negotiated a treaty with it on terms similar to those that Colombia had rejected.

The President did not start the revolution, but his treatment of the Colombians and his haste in recognizing the new Republic of Panama did his reputation a great deal of harm. If Roosevelt had understood the sensitivity of all Latin Americans to the United States' efforts to expand its influence in the Western Hemisphere, he would have moved more slowly and kept in mind that a powerful nation can seldom lose by treating weak neighbors with kindness and forbearance. In that case his canal would have been built almost as soon, and his country's problems in Latin America today would undoubtedly be less serious than they are. His chief fault—one out of character with his usual treatment of men on their merits—was his assumption that Latin Americans were inferior simply because they were weak, proud, and so sensitive that they sometimes acted irrationally.

He made the same mistake when he announced the Roosevelt Corollary to the Monroe Doctrine in his annual message to Congress on December 6, 1904. The Monroe Doctrine, a hallowed American policy dating from the 1820's, forbade any European power from taking over new territory in the Western Hemisphere. The President had become alarmed when some powers began putting great pressure on Caribbean nations that had failed to pay their debts—blockading their ports and even sinking their ships. Roosevelt declared that the United States would "exercise . . . international police power" in the area; that is, the United States would itself intervene in behalf of other powers to collect unpaid international obligations. He had dramatically changed the Monroe Doctrine from a ban against European intervention to a justification of American intervention.

Once again, the President acted only to protect the United States against possible establishment of European bases in the Caribbean. He never used this corollary as an excuse for taking over a Latin American country. But it aroused fears of Yankee imperialism in Latin America that have never entirely disappeared.

By 1904 Roosevelt had established himself solidly as the most popular man in the nation. People thought of him familiarly as "T.R." or "Teddy" and bragged about his "big stick" policy in international affairs and his "trust busting" at home. His Square Deal slogan attracted millions of voters. That November he won a second term in his own right, defeating the Democratic candidate, Alton B. Parker, by a majority of two and a half million votes. "Parker ran for the Presidency against Theodore Roosevelt," one humorist noted, "and was defeated by acclamation."

CHAPTER 8

THE SECOND TERM

WHEN ROOSEVELT BEGAN HIS SECOND TERM in March, 1905, the prospects for a successful administration were excellent. The President had the personal endorsement of the voters and the self-confidence, born of experience, that he could run the complex machinery of the Federal Government effectively. The tide of history was also running in his favor. The country was prosperous, which made people generous and hopeful but impatient with its defects and willing to make sacrifices to improve their society. They were sure America could solve any problem and make itself the greatest nation in the history of the world. By 1905 these conditions, combined with Roosevelt's popularity, had produced some changes in the make-up of Congress. The progressive element was strengthened, and even conservatives were beginning to feel that they must make concessions to the reform spirit.

The President sensed the new atmosphere in Washington and throughout the country, and he was eager to take advantage of it. Over the next four years he pressed continually for reform. The results were impressive. In passing the 1906 Hepburn Act, Congress imposed new, tight controls on the operations of railroads. The act gave the Interstate Commerce Commission power to regulate freight and passenger rates more effectively and to inspect corporation financial records. It also made it illegal for railroads to hand out free passes to politicians and other persons whose influence they courted.

Congress also passed a pure food and drug act and a meat-inspection law. These measures were designed to prevent the misleading labeling of goods and the selling of dangerous drugs or diseased foods. Roosevelt instituted several more important antitrust suits against monopolistic corporations.

He also shrewdly used his executive power to conserve the natural resources of the nation. Perhaps his greatest achievement in this area was his success in dramatizing the importance of conservation. Now that the frontier had disappeared, he saw the growing danger of exhausting the forests, mineral resources, and other natural assets of the soil. He placed more than 150 million acres of forest land in national parks and other reserves so that they could not be destroyed by lumber companies, and he called a three-day conference of governors and other national leaders that led to a vast program of state conservation.

By 1908 Roosevelt had become much more liberal in his approach to many national problems. He was asking Congress for Federal income and inheritance taxes, for laws further protecting the rights of workingmen, and for measures strictly regulating the activities of large corporations.

The achievements of his second term were not made

easily, however, despite the new temper of the people. Many conservatives continued to oppose every change; but more advanced progressives demanded still more drastic reforms. Always seeking practical results, Roosevelt carefully picked his way between these two extremes.

From Roosevelt's viewpoint, the nation was a vast collection of special interests: farmers, industrial workers, businessmen, lawyers, artists, doctors. He believed that men with similar objectives should organize themselves in groups to put forward their demands and that the government, under his leadership, should balance these demands one against the other to arrive at the general good. He distrusted anyone who expected to get everything he wanted. He denounced standpat conservatives and "malefactors of great wealth," who would make no concessions to the needs of the poor, but he also attacked the "lunatic fringe" among the reformers, who would not concede that other men's ideas deserved consideration. As one historian put it, Roosevelt "stood close to the center and bared his teeth at the conservatives of the right and the liberals of the extreme left."

This attitude won Roosevelt many enemies. Although the average man, who viewed politics from afar, tended to cheer everything he did, those who were more involved in the actions of the government often fought him bitterly. The accomplishments of his second term were made only by using every political trick he could think of.

By this time he had indeed become a master politician. His special talent was in forcing conservatives in Congress to go along with new ideas. Some of his opponents he convinced by argument. Others he kept in line by offering them political rewards such as jobs for friends and supporters and Federal grants for projects desired by voters in their districts. His cleverest technique, however, was to hold the threat of still more extreme proposals over their heads to make them accept his own programs. For example, when standpat Republican senators balked at the bill increasing the power of the Interstate Commerce Commission over railroads, the President threatened to propose lowering the tariff on manufactured goods. When they objected to the meat-inspection bill, he announced that if the moderate measure he was backing was not passed, he would release to the public a secret report on the filthy conditions in slaughterhouses. This report, he indicated, was so shocking that its publication would cause the people to demand an even stricter law.

Roosevelt did not hesitate to exaggerate in such situations or to embarrass his opponents. When he wanted Congress to create a bureau of corporations with power to investigate the activities of big business, he helped the bill along by announcing that John D. Rockefeller, multimillionaire head of the notorious Standard Oil trust, was opposed to the idea. Thus, congressmen who objected to the new bureau were made to appear henchmen of the widely hated Rockefeller, whether in fact they were or not.

Both in his methods and in his objectives, Roosevelt sought immediate gains, trusting to the future to take care of itself. As time passed, the methods began to work less effectively. When one objective was achieved he tended to seek another, usually a more progressive one. This moved him gradually out of the political center. Thus his talent for balancing conflicting forces was put to increasingly severe strains. By the last year of his second term, conservatives were digging in their heels and resisting all his tricks and pressures. They argued that they had made enough concessions to progress. The country needed a breathing spell, they claimed, time to digest the advances of the past seven years. Roosevelt continued to demand new legislation, but few important new laws were passed. Describing the situation with typical humor, he said, "The period of stagnation continued to rage with uninterrupted violence."

CHAPTER 9

AFRICAN SAFARI

AT THE TIME OF HIS ELECTION IN 1904, Roosevelt had ruled out a third term. In 1908, though he did not wish to run again for President, he was easily able to control the choice of his successor. The man he picked was William Howard Taft of Ohio, a large, jovial fellow whose geniality and lack of aggressiveness concealed a sharp mind and first-rate administrative ability.

Taft had been a judge in Ohio and had also sat on the Federal bench. In addition, he had served as governor of the Philippine Islands and Secretary of War in Roosevelt's cabinet. His loyal support of the Square Deal reforms appealed to progressives, yet he retained the confidence of conservative Republican leaders. He was nominated without serious opposition and then went on to win the 1908 election handily, defeating by more than a million votes the Democratic candidate, William Jennings Bryan. After two earlier defeats, Bryan was making his final bid for the Presidency.

If he remained nearby, Roosevelt wisely concluded, he would overshadow the new President and make it difficult for him to organize a strong administration. As soon as the inauguration ceremonies were over, Roosevelt departed for Africa to hunt big game and collect specimens for the Smithsonian Institution. He was accompanied by his twenty-year-old son Kermit and a team of scientists. The good wishes of most Americans and the relieved sighs of a handful of reactionaries went along in his wake. His friend Henry Cabot Lodge wrote that the public was following his adventures "with the absorbed interest of a boy who reads *Robinson Crusoe* for the first time." The disgruntled J. P. Morgan was supposed to have said that he hoped the first lion Roosevelt encountered in Africa would "do his duty."

The African safari was another great adventure for Roosevelt, one to rank with his days as a cowboy in the Dakota Territory and as a Rough Rider during the Spanish-American War. The expedition employed a small army of 260 porters and guides, but it was no luxury tour. Most of the porters were needed for transporting the equipment of the naturalists and taxidermists who were doing museum work. Although he enjoyed every moment of the trip, Roosevelt endured real hardships and faced serious dangers. His energy seemed limitless. After a hard day's hunting, he would sit up late (often surrounded by mosquito netting and wearing heavy gloves as protection against insect bites) writing an account of his adventures for *Scribner's Magazine*. The articles were later printed in a book, *African Game Trails*.

On April 21, 1909, having disembarked in British East Africa at Mombasa, Roosevelt proceeded by rail to the Kapiti plains, riding much of the time on the cowcatcher of the locomotive. From there his safari moved into the big-game country. By mid-May he had shot six lions, two giraffes, a hippo, a zebra, many varieties of antelope, and a rhinoceros, "which charged viciously, and might have done mischief," Roosevelt explained, "had it not been for a lucky rather than a skillful shot which dropped him at fourteen paces." After further hunting, the party visited Nairobi, capital of British East Africa, where Roosevelt was royally entertained by British officials. Then the safari continued southward. Roosevelt became increasingly proud of his son Kermit, who, like his father, had been a timid boy but who now was "altogether too bold," killing a rhinoceros, for example, at point-blank range "on a plain as bare as a billiard table."

At Lake Naivasha, Roosevelt hunted hippopotamuses in shallow water from a rowboat and wrote this graphic account of one kill: ". . . as it rushed forward with its huge jaws stretched to their threatening utmost, I fired right between them, whereat it closed them with the clash of a sprung bear trap; and then, when under the punishment it swerved for a moment, I hit it at the base of the ear, a brain shot which dropped it in its tracks."

Next the tireless former President headed toward the slopes of Mount Kenya for elephant. During the fall he traveled to Lake Victoria, Lake Albert, and then into the Belgian Congo, where he shot nine rare white rhinos. By December the party had collected over 11,000 specimens, including over 500 examples of big game, "the most noteworthy collection of big animals that has ever come out of Africa," Roosevelt proudly wrote.

Yet along with all this activity, Roosevelt still found time to read, to write many letters, and to work on his own book. "I am too old a man to be satisfied merely with a hunter's life," he explained. From Mount Kenya he had written the historian George Otto Trevelyan about the relative merits of two famous nineteenth-century British historians, Thomas Carlyle and Thomas B. Macaulay. He read and then wrote a review of a current American best seller, William Allen White's *A Certain Rich Man,* and he commented shrewdly on the books chosen by President Charles W. Eliot of Harvard for his famous Five-Foot Shelf of the world's great literature. "It is all right as *a* list," Roosevelt wrote, "but as *the* list it strikes me as slightly absurd." And he went on in great detail to mention important books that Eliot had ignored.

The hunt continued, moving by slow stages down the White Nile to Khartoum in the Anglo-Egyptian Sudan. There the expedition broke up in March, 1910. Mrs. Roosevelt joined her husband at Khartoum, and after going on to Cairo, they sailed across the Mediterranean to Europe.

Everywhere in Europe, Roosevelt received a tumultuous welcome. The sovereigns of Italy, Austria-Hungary, Belgium, Holland, Germany, and Great Britain all entertained him. Most of these monarchs did not greatly impress him. Their jobs were like that of an American Vice-President, he concluded; personally, "They were like other human beings in that the average among them was not very high as regards intellect and force. . . ." At a great dinner at Buckingham Palace in London, attended by eight reigning monarchs, Roosevelt was the center of attention. "The kings have been fairly scrambling for a share in his conversation," an American diplomat who was present reported. "I have never attended a more hilarious banquet in my life," Roosevelt himself said. "I have never seen so many knights. . . .

When I met a little bewizened person known as the King of Greece, he fairly wept out his troubles to me."

In addition to the many formal receptions, Roosevelt also lectured at Oxford and Cambridge universities and talked with important European political leaders. In Sweden he accepted the Nobel Peace Prize, awarded to him for his work in helping to end the Russo-Japanese War in 1905. At last his long trip drew to a close. "Ugh!" he wrote. "I do dread getting back to America and having to plunge into this cauldron of politics."

CHAPTER 10

BULL MOOSE

THEODORE ROOSEVELT HAD SOUND REASONS for worry. William Howard Taft, in his opinion, had proved a failure as President. He lacked both Roosevelt's energy and his political skill, and once outside his former chief's magnetic influence, he had tended to become rather conservative. Progressive Republicans were soon criticizing him bitterly. First they accused him of selling out to big business by refusing to fight hard for tariff reduction. Then they were outraged by his failure to back Gifford Pinchot, chief of the United States Forest Service, when Pinchot became embroiled in a controversy over conservation policy with Taft's Secretary of the Interior, Richard A. Ballinger.

The complaints of the progressives were not entirely justified. Taft had managed to persuade Congress to lower some of the import duties on manufactured goods and had actually instituted far more antitrust suits than had the celebrated trust buster Roosevelt. And Pinchot, by adopting an insubordinate and arrogant attitude, had practically forced Taft to support Ballinger. Nevertheless, by the spring of 1910 the Taft administration was in serious political trouble. The Republican party was being torn apart by the conflict between its progressive wing and the conservatives, who were now being called the Old Guard.

The progressives counted on Roosevelt to take up their cause, while the Old Guard expected him to stand by Taft, whom he had, after all, personally chosen as his successor. Roosevelt, eager to keep his new place as a great world statesman, promised, upon his arrival in New York on June 18, 1910, to make no political statements for two months. But he found it difficult to avoid disputes and steer a middle course between warring party factions. His liberal convictions were steadily pushing him toward the progressives. Furthermore, he was beginning to feel that Taft, resentful because he knew he could not have become President without Roosevelt's help, actually wanted to break off their friendship in order to prove his independence.

Roosevelt also disapproved of Taft's vigorous trust-busting policy. More and more he had come to think that combinations of large corporations were necessary because of their efficiency. "Nothing of importance is gained by breaking up a huge inter-state industrial organization which has not offended otherwise than by its size," he now argued. Unlimited competition between companies making similar goods was not only impossible but undesirable, he insisted. Let the corporations grow big, and then protect the public by strict regulatory laws against the possible abuse of corporate power.

His dissatisfaction with Taft, together, of course, with

a revived ambition to become President again, finally led Roosevelt to announce in January, 1912, that he was a candidate for the Republican nomination.

In the fight to win delegates to the nominating convention, Roosevelt advanced an extremely radical program. He proposed to regulate big business closely, to pass new laws benefiting industrial workers and the poor, and to crack down on all forms of special privilege. He called this program the New Nationalism, which was an accurate title, since the central idea was to grant more power to the national government in order to protect and advance the general welfare. Conservatives, believing strongly in unrestricted individualism—"that government is best which governs least"—considered him practically a socialist.

Democratic party liberals, such as Governor Woodrow Wilson of New Jersey, also attacked the New Nationalism. Wilson, soon to become the Democratic presidential candidate, proposed a New Freedom, which sought to achieve the same goals that Roosevelt was seeking, without expanding the functions of the Federal Government. Wilson's idea was that direct controls were unnecessary. If the government simply established strict rules of fair behavior, free competition would protect society against monopoly and other forms of special privilege. For example, he took the trust-busting approach to the monopoly problem in contrast to Roosevelt's plan calling for detailed government regulation of the large corporations.

In the states where Republican convention delegates were chosen by the voters in primary elections, the popular Roosevelt was almost universally successful; even Ohio, Taft's home state, elected Roosevelt delegates. As is still the case, however, a majority of the delegates were chosen at state nominating conventions, which the professional politicians dominated. These politicians were mostly Taft backers. In some states the Taft men used shady means to elect convention delegates, and at the national convention, which opened June 18 in Chicago, Roosevelt's supporters challenged the right of these delegates to their seats. The Taft machine refused to listen seriously to the Roosevelt challengers. When it was clear that Taft controlled the convention, the Roosevelt delegates walked out, and Taft won the nomination easily.

Feeling that he had been cheated, Roosevelt then decided to organize a third party and run for President on his own. This was an understandable but unfortunate decision. If he had accepted defeat and remained in the Republican party, no doubt Taft would still have lost the election to Wilson; but afterward, Roosevelt and his progressives would probably have been able to gain control of the Republican organization. By forming a separate Progressive party, he siphoned off all the liberal sentiment from the Republican ranks, leaving only the Old Guard. The party became ultraconservative and remained so for more than a generation.

Roosevelt realized that he had no chance of actually winning the election. He ran partly for revenge and partly in order to educate the voters for future campaigns. His competitive spirit was also aroused, and he was fired by the enthusiasm of his followers, who made up in crusading spirit for their lack of numbers. At the Progressive nominating convention, held in Chicago in early August, 1912, the delegates sang inspirational songs like "Onward Christian Soldiers" and shook the hall with cheers for nearly an hour when Roosevelt appeared before them. His acceptance speech was a triumph. He called it a "Confession of Faith." After outlining his program in detail, he closed with these words: "But win or lose, we shall not falter. . . . Our cause is based on the eternal principles of righteousness; and even though we who now lead may for the time fail, in the end the cause itself shall triumph. . . . We stand at Armageddon, and we battle for the Lord."

When questioned about his ability to undertake a strenuous campaign, Roosevelt said he felt "as strong as a bull moose," a favorite expression of his. The name stuck, and the bull moose became a symbol for the Progressive party, just as the elephant and the donkey had come to symbolize the Republican and Democratic parties.

The campaign was equally exciting, marked indeed by

one of the most dramatic incidents in American political history. On October 14, as he emerged from his hotel in Milwaukee on the way to make a speech, Roosevelt was shot in the chest by an anti–third-term fanatic. Luck alone saved his life, for the bullet had passed through his eyeglass case and the thick manuscript of his speech before smashing a rib and coming to rest just short of his right lung. The force of the blow knocked him over, but he sprang to his feet at once. "Stand back," he shouted as bystanders rushed forward to assault the would-be assassin. "Don't hurt the man!"

The wound was not fatal, but of course Roosevelt could not have known this at the moment. Doctors were summoned and tried to take him to a hospital, but he refused to go. "I will make this speech or die," he said. "It is one thing or the other." Off he went to the Milwaukee Auditorium, clutching a bloody handkerchief to his breast. ". . . I have just been shot," he explained to the hushed crowd, "but it takes more than that to kill a Bull Moose. . . . I want you to understand that I am ahead of the game, anyway. . . . Don't waste any sympathy on me. I have had an A-1 time in life and I am having it now. . . ." Then he proceeded to speak for almost an hour about the issues of the day before finally consenting to go to the hospital to have the wound treated.

Roosevelt recovered quickly, in time to make one more major address and several talks before Election Day, but his courage and popularity could not overcome the combined opposition of the two major parties. When the votes were counted in November, Woodrow Wilson was found to be the winner. Running with the support of a united Democratic party, he received 6,286,124 votes. But Roosevelt's achievement had been remarkable. Without the support of a major party, and attacked by conservative Republicans as well as by the Democrats, he nevertheless collected 4,126,020 votes. Taft, despite the prestige of the Presidency, got 3,483,922 votes. A fourth candidate, the socialist labor-leader Eugene V. Debs, received nearly one million votes, double his showing in 1908.

Many enthusiastic Bull Moosers believed that Roosevelt's excellent showing in 1912 meant that their organization would soon replace the Republican party in the American two-party system. Roosevelt himself, being a shrewd political analyst, had his doubts, and he was correct. In the first place, it was a one-man party. Although many Progressives ran for office in 1912, only eighteen were elected to Congress; Roosevelt's personal popularity did not rub off on most candidates. There were other problems too. The party lacked money and the solid network of loyal workers that was needed to keep a national organization running.

Most important, however, Woodrow Wilson quickly stole most of the Progressives' thunder. His New Freedom program was very appealing to the voters, and he proved to be even more effective than Roosevelt had been at getting Congress to enact his proposals into law. The Progressives were also hurt by internal conflicts, especially by one concerning the knotty problem of the great trusts. One group, led by George W. Perkins, an ex-banker who had contributed a great deal of money to the party, argued for Roosevelt's idea of allowing corporations to combine into monopolies because big business organizations were efficient. Another group insisted upon the trust-busting approach.

Roosevelt sided with the Perkins forces, but he seemed to be losing interest in domestic politics. In October, 1913, he left the United States for South America, where he was scheduled to make a series of speeches and do some hunting. In the course of these South American travels, he learned of the existence, in Brazil, of a great stream called the River of Doubt, which had never been explored. It ran through wild, dangerous country, but Roosevelt decided to try to trace its entire course. The Brazilian government, flattered by his interest, mounted a full-scale expedition under the command of Roosevelt and Colonel Candido Rondon to survey the region and collect specimens.

The party, which included Kermit Roosevelt and a number of naturalists, first hunted along the southern border of Brazil. There, Roosevelt shot many interesting animals, including the giant anteater, which he described as "the size of a bear, with a tail like an enormous skunk," and the white-lipped peccary, a savage wild boar, whose teeth "clatter . . . like castanets." Then, with a crew of Brazilian paddlers for their seven dugout canoes, the explorers began the descent of the River of Doubt on February 27, 1914. For forty-eight days they did not see another human being.

The African trip had been exciting but relatively comfortable. This voyage was hazardous in the extreme. Vicious mosquitoes and other insects tortured them; everyone came down with tropical fever; the river was full of whirlpools and rapids. Five of the canoes were smashed against rocks and destroyed by the turbulent waters. Supplies had to be abandoned; food ran short. One man was drowned, and one paddler went mad, killing his boss and fleeing into the jungle.

On March 27, Roosevelt gashed his leg while trying to save a dugout from capsizing. The wound became infected; wracked by fever, he ran a temperature of 105. At one point, feeling that he was becoming a burden to his companions, he even urged them to push on without him and leave him to die in the jungle.

Of course they refused to do so, and finally the party

reached civilization—some rubber plantations at the point where the river flows into a branch of the Amazon. Roosevelt had traveled nearly one thousand miles along a river that no man had ever seen before. The Brazilian government promptly changed its name to Rio Roosevelt, but since Portuguese-speaking people have some difficulty pronouncing that name, the river is commonly known as Rio Teodoro.

In the course of this adventure, Roosevelt had lost fifty-seven pounds, and although he appeared to make a quick recovery from his injuries, he never again regained his full strength. He was stricken periodically with fever, and undoubtedly the grueling experiences he endured hastened his death considerably. Characteristically, however, Roosevelt shrugged off the hardships that most men of fifty-five would never have risked. "We have had a hard and somewhat dangerous but very successful trip," he explained.

Within a month he was back in the United States and complaining of the "very disheartening condition" of the political situation. He spoke of the "malignance of the

Republican leaders" and the "wild-eyed folly" of some of his own Progressives. He brushed aside suggestions that he run for governor of New York that fall.

Then, early in August, 1914, World War I broke out in Europe. For the rest of his life, this great cataclysm was to be the central fact of Theodore Roosevelt's existence.

CHAPTER II

WARRIOR WITHOUT A WAR

ROOSEVELT'S FIRST REACTION TO THE NEWS of war in Europe was, like that of most Americans, somewhat confused. To a country still isolated from a Europe of dynasties, international rivalries, and secret diplomacy, there seemed little to distinguish the Central Powers—Germany and Austria-Hungary—from the Allies—Britain, France, and Russia. A common language and other cultural ties made many Americans sympathetic to the Allied cause, but a large German-American population tended to favor the Central Powers.

When the Germans attacked Belgium simply because the tiny kingdom lay across a desirable invasion route into France, Roosevelt along with neutrals the world over was shocked and angered. At the same time, however, his admiration of strength and his belief that war was the proper final solution to conflicts between nations led him to look at the invasion cold-bloodedly. "When giants are engaged in a death wrestle," he said, "they are certain to trample on whoever gets in the way. . . ." As a patriotic American he also felt obliged to stand behind the President in a crisis, and Wilson had quickly declared the neutrality of the United States. Roosevelt therefore did not come out publicly for any positive American action during the first months of the conflict.

However, his emotional ties were with England and France, and the more he learned about Germany's ruthless assault on Belgium the more he began to feel that at least a strong official protest would have been in order. More important, as he considered the long-range possibilities involved in the war, he came to think that the United States' interests required that Germany be defeated. If the Kaiser's armies conquered Europe, he believed that Germany might make an alliance with Japan and that these two powers might possibly attack America's east and west coasts. As early as October, 1914, he was calling for a great increase in the Army and Navy in order to prepare against this possibility.

President Wilson rejected the demand of men like Roosevelt for what was called preparedness. He argued that the war was none of America's business. If the United States maintained a policy of strict neutrality, both sides might then agree to let the President act as a mediator and might settle their conflict peacefully.

Roosevelt soon decided that Wilson was either secretly pro-German or personally a coward, and he began to attack the President harshly in public speeches. By 1915 he was eager to have America declare war on Germany, but knowing that the people were not ready for this step, he spoke only about preparedness and economic aid to the Allied powers. His public utterances became even more belligerent, however, after a German submarine sank the British ocean liner *Lusitania* in May, 1915. Nearly 1,200 civilians, including 128 Americans, were killed in this disaster. Dubbing the sinking "piracy . . . warfare against innocent men, women, and children," he called for strong retaliatory action. Wilson confined himself to paper protests and negotiations, and Roosevelt's contempt for the President mounted to new heights. In private letters he called Wilson's behavior "criminal from the standpoint of the national honor and interest" and referred to him as "that infernal skunk in the White House" and an "utterly selfish, utterly unpatriotic coward."

Roosevelt had pretty well abandoned any ambition to regain the Presidency in the 1916 election. Therefore he firmly expressed his own strong opinions. In his speeches and writings, he also attacked American neutrals, especially those of German descent who, while loyal to the United States, objected strongly to any policy that aided the Allies. Since such persons made up an enormous voting bloc, Roosevelt's uncompromising criticism of them was bad politics and certainly out of keeping with his usual policy of seeking compromise on controversial issues. He was determined, however, "to wake up our people to unpleasant facts by telling them unpleasant truths." He thus considered himself "impossible as a candidate," but he detested Wilson so much that he was willing to run if he could obtain the support of both the Progressives and the Republicans.

Of course the Progressives were eager to renominate him. So were many rank-and-file Republicans, for they realized that without Progressive votes their chances of defeating Wilson were very small. The two parties therefore adopted the strategy of holding their nominating conventions at the same time and in the same city, Chicago. They drafted practically identical programs, and their leaders conferred at length before allowing the presidential balloting to begin.

Roosevelt talked about his prospects with many prominent members of both organizations over a private telephone line between Chicago and his home at Oyster Bay, on Long Island. The conservative Republican leaders, unwilling to forgive him for having bolted their party in 1912, flatly refused to accept him as their candidate. The Progressives, on the other hand, would accept no one else. Roosevelt, however, was ready to support a number of other men, and he refused to run himself unless both parties nominated him. He was too old, he told his Progressive friends over the telephone, for another campaign against impossible odds. "There is a very wide difference . . . between making a young Colonel and a retired Major General lead a forlorn hope."

The Republicans finally went ahead and nominated Supreme Court Justice Charles Evans Hughes, a former governor of New York. The Progressives in turn nominated Roosevelt. He refused to accept, however. He disliked Hughes personally and feared he was not sufficiently in favor of preparedness. "We do not want to find that we have merely swapped Wilson for another Wilson with whiskers," he warned of the bearded justice. But when Hughes assured him about his attitude toward the war, Roosevelt endorsed him. "He will make a straight-out fight for preparedness and national defense," he said.

Roosevelt's abandonment of the Progressives effectively destroyed the party, but he was no longer very interested in domestic reform. He made many speeches for Hughes, although some Republican politicians worried that his attacks on pacifists and German-Americans were doing their candidate more harm than good. The Democratic campaign, stressing the fact that Wilson had managed to maintain the peace, had a powerful appeal to voters. By the narrowest of margins, Wilson was re-elected in November, 1916. Roosevelt was despondent. He had actually restrained his feelings during the campaign, never, for example, advocating the immediate declaration of war against Germany that he desired. Wilson's victory, largely won by the slogan "He kept us out of war," seemed to Roosevelt to indicate that a majority of the American people were cowards.

Actually, events were running in the direction Roosevelt wished. After the sinking of the *Lusitania* and other passenger vessels, Wilson's diplomatic pressures had eventually forced the Germans to stop submarine attacks on unarmed ships without warning. Early in 1917, however, the German high command persuaded the Kaiser that the only way to win the war was to torpedo every possible ship bringing supplies to the Allies. Once this strategy was announced, Wilson became convinced that the United States would have to fight not merely to protect American lives and property but to put an end to the long and dreadful conflict that was threatening to destroy civilization itself. On April 2, 1917, he asked Congress to declare war; four days later Congress did so.

By deciding to fight, the President was admitting that Roosevelt had been correct in calling Germany a menace to America. But the former Rough Rider wasted little time in gloating. He called upon the people to back Wilson to the hilt and threw himself wholeheartedly into the war effort. For months he had been planning to repeat his action of 1898 and raise a volunteer force. This time he had in mind raising an entire division of 25,000 men.

He realized that warfare had changed since 1898, that it was a bitter business fought in mud and trenches and required professional leadership. "The bronco-buster type will be very much lacking," he promised when describing his plan.

Roosevelt intended to get into the fight himself,

despite his age and declining health. "I wish respectfully to point out," he wrote Wilson's Secretary of War, Newton D. Baker, "that [as former President] I am a retired Commander in Chief of the United States Army and eligible to any position of command over American troops to which I may be appointed."

Shortly after war was declared, he went to Washington and had a long private conference with Wilson. He was eager to help in any way and expressed full support for Wilson's plan for universal military service—the draft. But he pleaded to be allowed to raise his volunteer division from men below and above draft age and take them to the front as soon as possible. Wilson apparently encouraged him, for Roosevelt left the meeting in a cheerful mood. A few days later, however, Secretary Baker informed him that his plan had been rejected. No force was to be sent overseas until detailed plans had been worked out, and then it must be commanded by "men . . . who have devoted their lives exclusively to the study and pursuit of military matters and have made a professional study of the recent changes in the art of war," Baker wrote. Roosevelt, who had no exaggerated faith in the ability of West Pointers, said that "a mutton-head, after an education at West Point—or Harvard—is a muttonhead still. . . ."

Roosevelt was not only disappointed, he was furious with Baker and Wilson. He pointed out to the Secretary of War that he had commanded a regiment in the most important battle fought by American troops in the last half century, that as a former Commander in Chief, he had "devoted much time and study and thought to the study of military and naval problems." Moreover, he argued, the prompt arrival of American volunteer troops at the front would provide the Allied armies with a great boost in their morale.

"If you don't know whether the governments of the Allies would like me to raise such a division and take it abroad at the earliest possible moment," he wrote to Baker, "I wish you would ask those governments yourself their feeling in the matter." He was actually right about those feelings. A number of Allied leaders told Wilson they thought Roosevelt's plan was excellent. Georges

WARRIOR WITHOUT A WAR

Clemenceau, soon to become premier of France, wrote the President that "there is in France one name which sums up the beauty of American intervention. It is the name of Roosevelt. . . ."

The frustrated former President pleaded again and again in long letters to Baker. He offered to raise two, then four, divisions, to accept a subordinate position among the commanding officers, but Baker rejected every suggestion. Roosevelt was destined to sit out the war on the sidelines.

Wilson would probably have been wise to accept Roosevelt's offer, perhaps with the proviso that Roosevelt himself remain in the United States. Wilson offered many reasons for not doing so, but his hatred of Roosevelt and his fear that the old Rough Rider would emerge from the war a still greater hero were probably central to his decision. ". . . the best way to treat Mr. Roosevelt," he said icily, "is to take no notice of him. That breaks his heart and is the best punishment that can be administered."

Although Roosevelt never forgave Wilson for this

slight, he did not let personal feelings interfere with his loyal support of the war. He wrote over a hundred newspaper articles and made dozens of speeches urging the people to throw their full energies into the struggle. Although he was in very poor health, suffering repeated attacks of the tropical fever he had caught in Brazil, he drove himself mercilessly. With his enthusiastic approval, all four of his sons volunteered, serving with distinction. The oldest, Theodore Jr., rose to the rank of lieutenant colonel and was both wounded and gassed. Archibald served as a captain of infantry and was twice wounded. Kermit saw action in France and in Mesopotamia. Quentin, the youngest, who was only twenty, became a pilot; he died in combat over Château-Thierry in July, 1918.

With himself and his sons so fully in the fight, Roosevelt had no patience with pacifists, and he lost his sense of balance in condemning anyone who disagreed with his stand. He attacked all things German, even demanding that American schools stop teaching the language. He temporarily lost much of his liberalism and tolerance, urging, for example, harsh treatment for workers who went on strike or for radicals who expressed disapproval of the war. This was inexcusable as well as uncharacteristic; it can only be explained in terms of his intense patriotism.

The former President's blasts at German-Americans were intended to hit only those who put Germany before America, but they sometimes struck others too. "I have had to make war with the black flag hoisted against the pro-Germans and German-Americans," he explained to the English writer Rudyard Kipling. He went on to draw a clear distinction between the two groups. "My own theory of dealing with them is perfectly simple. I exact from every man an absolutely undiluted Americanism, and if he gives it I care not a rap as to the land from which his father came or the creed he professes." This was the real Roosevelt speaking. In his public attacks, however, the confusion often remained; thus he contributed to the cruel treatment of many loyal German-Americans during the war.

Roosevelt assaulted Wilson violently whenever he felt

that the President was failing to carry on the war as vigorously as possible. He denounced the long delay in getting American troops into the battle, the snags that developed in the manufacture of planes and heavy artillery, and the ineffectiveness of the government's shipbuilding program. He also criticized Wilson for not taxing war profits more heavily, saying that it was necessary "to put a stop to the making of unearned and improper fortunes out of the war."

The President's wise and humane decision that the German people should not be punished after the German army had been defeated made Roosevelt furious. In the fall of 1918, when Allied victory at last seemed certain, he demanded unconditional surrender, with harsh peace terms fixed by the Allies. Wilson believed that real peace depended upon re-establishing friendly feelings among the warring nations. He wanted a quick end to the fighting, on generous terms, backed by a league of nations.

To Roosevelt, Wilson's peace program seemed mere sentimental foolishness. While not against a league of nations, provided that it was based on a firm military alliance among the victorious powers, he insisted that Germany be crushed and punished. "Let us dictate peace by the hammering guns and not chat about peace to the accompaniment of the clicking of typewriters," he said.

Of course Wilson, not Roosevelt, determined how the United States would deal with the Germans. On November 11, 1918, an armistice was signed by the powers, ending the fighting before the Allies had even penetrated German territory. A great peace conference was to be held in Paris to work out a settlement based on justice rather than on brute power.

CHAPTER 12

DEATH OF A GIANT

ROOSEVELT DID NOT LIVE TO DISCOVER THE fate of Wilson's idealistic peace plans. Had he lived, he would probably have been the next President of the United States. His hard-hitting attacks on Wilson's administration had won him the applause of Republicans as well as Progressives. All factions were eager to nominate him in 1920. The Republican who did run, Warren G. Harding of Ohio, easily defeated the Democratic candidate, James M. Cox, also of Ohio.

Long before the election, however, Roosevelt's health began to fail rapidly. He was suffering from inflammatory rheumatism. A month in the hospital helped little.

He returned, cheerful but in great pain, to his home at Oyster Bay in December, 1918. He was able to keep on writing and speaking out on public issues, preaching "one-hundred percent Americanism" and trying to hold the Republican party together for the coming fight against Wilson and the Democrats. By the evening of January 5, 1919, he was so weak his personal servant, James Amos, had to help him into bed. In the predawn dark of January 6, he died peacefully in his sleep, at the age of sixty.

How can we sum up the life of this remarkable man? His direct achievements as a statesman do not seem so large today as they did during his lifetime. The domestic reforms of his Square Deal were overshadowed by those of Wilson's New Freedom and even more so by the New Deal of his distant cousin Franklin D. Roosevelt in the 1930's. His aggressive foreign policy was shortsighted, although based on hard truths that must never be forgotten about the nature of power. Roosevelt failed to realize that small nations are as much entitled to respect as great powers and that world public opinion is a tremendous force in international affairs. Furthermore, Roosevelt's egotism, his glorification of war, and his simple faith in his own righteousness now appear adolescent and arrogant.

Yet if one looks beyond the particular issues that Roosevelt dealt with, he emerges as the first modern President and a great statesman. He recognized that the people, expecting the President to guard the national interest, were ready to see presidential power expanded whenever the need arose. He considered it his duty to attack problems, not merely to administer laws. He used his position at the center of the national stage to call the public's attention to these problems so that, under his leadership, the whole nation could mobilize its resources for the job of working out the solutions. Many persons during Roosevelt's lifetime, and later too, accused him of being only a halfhearted liberal. His willingness to settle so often for half a loaf annoyed them. They forgot, however, that he inspired millions of Americans to adopt a liberal point of view and to accept their responsibility as individuals to try to help their less fortunate countrymen achieve a better life.

Roosevelt possessed intelligence of a very high order. The evidence of this is overwhelming, although, having so many interests and being over-confident of his own opinions, he sometimes made shaky snap judgments and failed to penetrate deeply into complicated questions. Some, but by no means all, of the books he wrote were extremely superficial. His literary gift, however, surely approached genius; his command of language, so vivid and colorful, makes everything he wrote interesting. This is especially true of his thousands of personal letters, written to statesmen and children, to scholars and men of action.

The enormous variety of his activities—his curiosity, his eagerness to learn, his ability to appreciate the value of new ideas—all testify to his great intelligence. A description of all his interests would fill many pages; any attempt to list the books he read in his lifetime would fill a volume.

While President, he took jujitsu lessons from a Japanese expert. Becoming fascinated by the art, he began to wonder whether a first-rate American wrestler could defeat a jujitsu specialist. He arranged a match in the White House between his instructor and the American middleweight wrestling champion. The result, he discovered, "was very interesting." The American had no trouble getting the Japanese on his back, but within a couple of minutes the Japanese had obtained holds that would have enabled him to choke his opponent to death or at least break his arm. "Wrestling," Roosevelt explained in a letter to Kermit, "is simply a sport with rules almost as conventional as those of tennis, while jujitsu is really meant for practice in killing or disabling an adversary." The incident, unimportant in itself, reveals fully Roosevelt's intense, analytical curiosity and his determination to discover truth. Hundreds of similar examples could be offered.

Above all, Roosevelt stands out as a great human being, one whose faults merely emphasize his virtues. His personal triumph over fear and physical weakness was only a small part of his achievement. His charm, his warmth, his love of life, along with his understanding that unhappiness, pain, and even death are part of life, all mark him as a truly exceptional person. Historian Elting E. Morison, who has edited his correspondence, points out that everything Roosevelt did, he did with all his might. He lived every day as though it were his last, not out of the fear of death, but in the belief that life was a precious gift.

He was indeed too prone to praise himself and his accomplishments, but this was part of his general enthusiasm for life; he was as free with praise of others as of himself. Fame and success never turned his head, and he always believed that every man should be treated on his merits, without regard for race, creed, or social position. His remarkable relationships with children were connected with this quality. Life at Sagamore Hill, the Roosevelt home at Oyster Bay, was a continual round of fascinating activities for the younger members of the family, first for his own children, then for a growing horde of grandchildren. Sports of every kind, nature study, storytelling, filled each day, bright or rainy, and Roosevelt was always in the middle of the crowd, not as an elder directing the show, but as one of the players. There was a boyish element in him that he never lost, even as President.

Although Roosevelt demanded a great deal of his children, he never, like some proud parents, tried to dominate them or push them ahead in order to boast about their achievements. His many letters to his sons and daughters reflect their relationship perfectly; he was their friend, eagerly communicating his experiences and ideas in phrases they could understand and enjoy. He shared his life with them, giving advice and support when needed, but above all treating them with the respect that is the highest form of parental love.

In sum, the chief virtue of Roosevelt the man, and the key to understanding his appeal to millions of Americans was his marvelous blend of love and sternness. He was the hunter who most admired his prey at the moment he squeezed the trigger. He had a powerful sense of duty but an equally solid awareness that life was a game; he tempered an unyielding moral code with a fundamental tolerance. He threw himself into everything he did without restraint but never took himself too seriously; he was egotistical but not pompous, not stuffy, not vain.

Shortly after he received the news that Quentin had been shot down over France, he told a friend, "If all our four sons should be killed, their mother and I would feel that, even although we were crushed by the blow, we would rather have it that way than not have had them go." Yet to another friend, the novelist Edith Wharton, he wrote, "There is no use my writing about Quentin; for I should break down if I tried. His death is heartbreaking." And a family servant observed him at Sagamore Hill, an open book in his lap, gazing blindly out into space and mumbling, "Poor Quinikins!" When only a few months later, the father himself died, the finest tribute paid him was the awareness, expressed by all who commented on his passing, of this noble mixture of courage and compassion.

TEDDY ROOSEVELT
PHOTO ALBUM

The Roosevelt family at their home in Sagamore Hill. From left to right: Quentin, TR, Theodore, Jr., Archibald, Alice, Kermit, Mrs. Roosevelt (Edith), and Ethel.

Roosevelt as a rancher in the Dakota Territories in 1885.

*Roosevelt and his Rough Riders at the top of
San Juan Hill, Cuba, July 1898.*

TR operating a steam shovel during the construction of the Panama Canal in 1906.

Roosevelt was the first American president to act as a world leader. He won a Nobel Peace Prize in 1906 for his efforts to end the war between Japan and Russia.

TR giving a speech from the back of a train in Eugene, Oregon in 1911.

Index

Roosevelt, Theodore:

administrative skills of,
81–84

on African safari, 103–7

assassination attempt on,
116–17

as assistant secretary of
Navy, 35–40

birth of, 2

bodybuilding by, 4–6,
142–43

books by, 2–3, 7, 19, 35, 44,
104

childhood of, 2–5

and Civil Service
Commission, 24–28

and Congress, 75, 79, 82,
96–97, 99–100

Dakota ranch of, 16–22

death of, 139

early political interests of,
8–13

European travel of, 107–8

family background of, 2–3

and foreign policy, 88–93,
139–40

gubernatorial campaign,
50–51

gubernatorial nomination,
49

health problems of, 3, 120,
134, 138–39

as hero, 44, 47, 66, 133

hunting, 6–7, 19–20, 71–72,
103–7, 119–20, 144

legacy of, 139–45

mayoral campaign (1886),
23–24

as New York assemblyman,
10–13, 15–16

as New York governor,
51–60, 61–62

Nobel Peace Prize to, 108

personal traits of, 1, 6, 7, 10,
16–17, 48, 50, 51, 54,
80–81, 140–45

ABOUT THE AUTHOR

Well-known biographer John Garraty is the author of dozens of books on American history. His works include *The American Nation* and *The Reader's Companion to American History*. He is also the editor of *The American National Biography*, a reference work of 17,500 biographies that was ten years in the making. Garraty was the Gouverneur Morris Professor Emeritus of History at Columbia University and has served as president of the Society of American Historians.

BOOKS IN THIS SERIES

Admiral Richard Byrd: Alone in the Antarctic
BY PAUL RINK

Alexander the Great
BY JOHN GUNTHER

Amelia Earhart: Flying Solo
BY JOHN BURKE

The Barbary Pirates
BY C. S. FORESTER

Behind Enemy Lines: A Young Pilot's Story
BY H. R. DEMALLIE

Ben Franklin: Inventing America
BY THOMAS FLEMING

General George Patton: Old Blood and Guts
BY ALDEN HATCH

George Washington: Frontier Colonel
BY STERLING NORTH

Geronimo: Wolf of the Warpath
BY RALPH MOODY

Invasion: The Story of D-Day
BY BRUCE BLIVEN, JR.

John Paul Jones: The Pirate Patriot
BY ARMSTRONG SPERRY

Lawrence of Arabia
BY ALISTAIR MACLEAN

Path to the Pacific: The Story of Sacagawea
BY NETA LOHNES FRAZIER

The Sinking of the Bismarck: The Deadly Hunt
BY WILLIAM SHIRER

The Stouthearted Seven: Orphaned on the Oregon Trail
BY NETA LOHNES FRAZIER

Teddy Roosevelt: American Rough Rider
BY JOHN A. GARRATY

✳ STERLING POINT BOOKS